Thi   e
rea   y
and   t
you   d,
alw   d,'s
con
by   s
me
and

PORTUGUESE PHRASE BOOK

A. Canavarro, L. Coleman
and R. Nash Newton

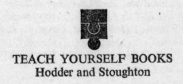

TEACH YOURSELF BOOKS
Hodder and Stoughton

First printed 1980

Copyright © 1980
A. Canavarro, L. Coleman and R. Nash Newton

Published in the USA by David McKay & Co. Inc., 750 Third Avenue, New York, NY 10017, USA.

ISBN 0 340 236973

Printed and bound in Great Britain
for Hodder and Stoughton paperbacks,
a division of Hodder and Stoughton Ltd,
Mill Road, Dunton Green, Sevenoaks, Kent
(Editorial Office: 47 Bedford Square, London, WC1B 3DP)
by Richard Clay (The Chaucer Press) Ltd, Bungay, Suffolk

Contents

Using this Phrase Book

In this phrase book, we do not set out to teach you the full grammar and vocabulary necessary for holding a long conversation. Basic words and phrases will help to make you feel more at home and will create goodwill among the people of the country you are visiting, even though they may speak fluent English themselves!

These phrases, coupled with appropriate gestures and signs (such as pointing to items in a shop) should ensure that you will be understood perfectly well.

As you will see, the book is divided into sections each dealing with everyday situations. You will also see that many of these sections repeat the same words and phrases. This means that you do not have to master a great number of new expressions in order to communicate adequately. And if you need a quick translation of a single word, there is a Reference Section and an alphabetical list of words at the back of the book.

Next to each phrase or word you will find the phonetic equivalent, the key to which is on page 4. Do remember, however, that accurate pronunciation alone is only half the battle: an appropriate gesture (or grimace) will help convey what you really mean!

An asterisk * on the left of a phrase means that this is a phrase you will need to understand but not to say yourself, *e.g.* 'Have you got anything to declare?'

We have tried to make the phrase book as comprehensive and yet as simple as possible. If you follow it carefully, it should help to make your stay in Portugal and Brazil enjoyable and carefree!

Pronunciation Guide*

The thing to remember about pronouncing Portuguese is that there is a strong tendency to 'swallow' any syllable which is not stressed. This is especially obvious when the word ends with an unstressed vowel: often the vowel is not pronounced at all.

If you look at the following key to Portuguese sounds, you will be able to pronounce words intelligibly, but it is worth mentioning a few important general rules here first.

Each word has one main stressed syllable and this we've shown in capital letters. Words ending in a, e, o and m are stressed on the next to last syllable *e.g.* **casa** KAza. All other words are stressed on the last syllable *e.g.* **papel** paPEL. Words which are exceptions to this rule have the stressed syllable marked with an accent, *e.g.* **América**, aMAYreeka. (If a word only consists of one syllable it is automatically stressed.) For example, the word **'tempo'** (weather) is transcribed TEMpoo. You must remember, however, that the final 'oo' is spoken very rapidly and is sometimes hard to catch when you are listening to a native speaker.

A final 'e', as in **'tarde'** (afternoon), is often not pronounced at all. In this case we transcribe it tard. Where the unstressed 'e' is sounded we transcribe it as ə. This is a very common sound in English so don't be put off by its unfamiliar appearance. It's the sound in 'the' when we say it quickly in a sentence. We have put it in the words where it is physically difficult NOT to pronounce it, *e.g.* **'chaves'** (keys), SHAvəsh.

Sometimes an unstressed 'a' is pronounced as ə, simply because the word is being spoken so quickly. For example, in **'salão'** (lounge) the first 'a' is hardly sounded at all and it will

---

* People interested in following this phrasebook with a view to speaking Portuguese in Brazil, should look at the section on Brazilian Portuguese pronunciation, after the Basic Grammar Guide.

sound like s'lowng. We have still transcribed it as an 'a' but remember not to give it anything like the same force as the stressed 'a'. If you think of the way the English pronounce the name Tamara, you will see that this Portuguese rule is in fact very similar to our own: təMARə.

Accents

There are four accents in Portuguese. They are all transcribed into their phonetic equivalents throughout the book, so just for your interest, here is what they mean:

The acute accent (e.g. é) is used to indicate a stressed syllable, and therefore a more open sound, *e.g.* **América** (aMAYreeka). It is also used to differentiate between two words which would otherwise look the same. *E.g.*

| é | (is) (ay) | and e | (and) (ə) |
| dá | (give) (dA) | and da | (of) (da) |

The circumflex (e.g. fôr) also indicates a more open sound.

E.g. **mês** (month) (maysh) and **pôr** (to put) (pohr)

The tilde (e.g. não) indicates a nasal sound, so whenever you see it, speak the vowel through your nose, as if there is an 'ng' sound after it.

E.g. **não** (no, not) (nowng), **são** (they are) (sowng), **manhã** (morning) (manYÃ).

The cedilla under the c (e.g. coração) before a, o and u softens the usual 'k' sound to an 's' sound.

E.g. **calças** (trousers) (KALsash).

This guide gives you the approximate English equivalent of sounds. You will appreciate that, as in Britain, people have different accents depending on which part of the country they come from, so we have tried to give you a simplified code which should make you easily understood wherever you go. To achieve the best results, first read the description of each phrase through slowly and carefully, then try reading it aloud at natural speaking speed.

The sounds in this guide are based on European Portuguese. They are, generally speaking, the same in Brazilian Portuguese, but for specific differences see the section on Brazilian Portuguese after the Basic Grammar Guide.

Consonants

Letter	Description	Symbol	Example
b	As in English.	b	
c	Before a, o, u, as in English.	k	casa KAza
	Before e and i, as the English s.	s	centro SENtroo
ç	Before a, o, u, as the English s.	s	almoço alMOsoo
d	As in English.	d	
f	As in English.	f	
g	Before a, o, u, as the English g in 'good'.	g	logo LOgoo
	Before e and i, like the s sound in 'measure'.	zh	longe lonzh

Letter	Description	Symbol	Example
h	Always silent.		
j	Like the s sound in 'measure'.	zh	**já** zha
l	As in English.*	l	
m	As in English, except at the end of words. See section on Combinations of sounds.	m	
n	As in English.*	n	
p	As in English.	p	
q(u)	Before a, as in English.	kw	**qual** kwal
	Before e, omit the w sound.	k	**que** kə
r	More audible than in English, like the beginning of a rolled r.	r	
rr	When double in the middle of words, pronounced at the back of the throat; like the ch sound in 'loch', or a very heavy English h.	h	**carro** KAhoo
s	Before a vowel, as in English.	s	**seguir** səGEER
	Before another consonant and at the end of words, like the English sh.	sh	**esta** ESHta **camas** KAmash
	Between two vowels, like the English z.	z	**casa** KAza
t	As in English.	t	
v	As in English.	v	

* Except when followed by h. See following section on Combination of sounds.

Letter	Description	Symbol	Example
x	Depending on its position in the word.	ks	taxi TAKsee
		s	próximo PROSseemoo
		z	exame eeZAM
		sh	baixo BYshoo
z	As in English, however, at the end of words it becomes sh or zh.	z	fazer fəZAIR
		sh	vez vaysh
		zh	faz fazh

Vowels

a	More open than the English a, approaching ah. When it is not stressed it is very short, almost swallowed: think of the way we pronounce 'Tamara' in English, then exaggerate it.	a	casa KAza
e	Like the e in 'men' in English.	e	tempo TEMpoo
é} ê}	More open, like the sound in 'day' in English.	ay	é ay mês maysh
e	When unstressed, it is either pronounced like the e in 'butter' or disappears altogether.	ə	dá-me DA-mə chaves SHAvəsh tarde tard está shta
	Before r when stressed, like the sound in English 'air'.	air	perto PAIRtoo
	Sometimes sounds more like the English i, when unstressed at the beginning of words.	ee	eléctrico eeLEKtreekoo

Letter	Description	Symbol	Example
i	Like the ee in meet.	ee	lindo LEENdoo
	Before another vowel, very short, like the y in 'yet'.	y	cambio KAMByoo
o	As in 'hot'.	o	próximo PROSseemoo
	When unstressed, like the oo in 'foot'.	oo	lindo LEENdoo cobertor koobərTOR
ô	Like the English 'oh'.	oh	pôr pohr
u	Like the oo in 'foot'.	oo	custa KOOSHta

Combinations of sounds

Vowels

ães	A nasal y as in 'my'.	yng	pães pyngsh
ai	Like the y in 'my'.	y	mais mysh
ao} au	Like the ow in 'how', with more oo at the end.	Aoo	ao Aoo
	For convenience, in longer words we show it as ow.	ow	autocarro owtooKAhoo
ão	As above but nasalised, *i.e.* followed by the English 'ng' ending.	owng	não nowng
-am	At the end of words, nasalised.	ang	eram AIRang
ei	A strong ay as in 'day'.	ay	feira FAYra
eu	Two distinct sounds: English e and oo, with the stress on the e.	Eoo	seu SEoo
-em	At the end of words, a nasalised ay as in 'day'.	ayng	tem tayng
ões	An o followed by a nasalised e.	Oeng	cartões karTOengsh

Letter	Description	Symbol	Example
oi	As in English 'oil'.	oi	**noite** noit
ou	A long 'oh'.	oh	**sou** soh
ui	Like the English 'wee' with a nasal ending.	ween	**muito** MWEENtoo
um	A nasalised oo.	oong	**ums** oongsh

Consonants

nh	Like the 'ni' in English 'onion'.	Ny/nY (depending on stress)	**banho** BANyoo
lh	Like the 'lli' in English 'million'.	Ly/lY	**toalha** TWALya

A Basic Grammar Guide

Portuguese is not a difficult language for English-speaking people to learn, so here are some of the simpler grammar rules that you may need for everyday conversations:

Nouns

Unlike English, there are two groups of nouns: masculine and feminine. Nouns ending in **o** are masculine and those ending in **a** are feminine, *e.g.* **o saco** (the bag), **a casa** (the house or room). Others you just have to try and remember as you come across them. Pocket dictionaries usually give the gender of the noun (m. or f.) when they give the meaning.

Notice that the Portuguese word for 'the' changes according to the noun: **o saco** and **a casa**. (In this respect Portuguese *is* confusing: **a** does not mean 'a'!)

To express 'a(n)' you must use **um** or **uma**, *e.g.* **um saco** (a bag), **uma casa** (a house).

Plurals

Plurals of nouns and articles are formed by adding **s** after vowels or **es** after consonants. The most important exception to remember is that the final **m** in a word becomes **n** in the plural before the **s***. *E.g.*

uns sacos	(some bags)	**umas casas**	(some houses)
os sacos	(the bags)	**as casas**	(the houses)
a mulher	(the woman)	**as mulheres**	(the women)
***o homem**	(the man)	**os homens**	(the men)

Exceptions
Other irregular plural endings to note:

lição	(lesson)	lições
sinal	(sign)	sinais

Adjectives

These also agree with the noun they are describing, and usually go after it (and not before as in English):

o homem feio   (the ugly man)   a blusa preta   (the black blouse)
os homens feios   as blusas pretas

There is a list of useful adjectives on page 22. The ones that end in o must change to a before a feminine noun. The ones that end in e or a consonant do not change in the singular but in the plural they add s or es or have the same changes as the above noun exceptions.

Prepositions

Certain prepositions, such as de (of), em (in) and por (by) contract with the articles which follow them, *e.g.*

de before o becomes do	and	de before os becomes dos
de before a becomes da		de before as becomes das
em before o becomes no	and	em before os becomes nos
em before a becomes na		em before as becomes nas
por before o becomes pelo	and	por before os becomes pelos
por before a becomes pela		por before as becomes pelas

E.g. a blusa da menina 'the girl's blouse', os uniformes dos meninos 'the boys' uniforms'.

Possessives

To show possession, use the preposition **de** (of) before the possessor as in the examples above, and, more simply, as in **'a casa de João'** 'John's house'.

The words for 'my', 'your' etc. are easy to learn, but notice that they agree with the thing possessed and NOT with the person who possesses it:

	Masc.		*Fem.*	
my	**meu**	Meoo	**minha**	MEENya
your (familiar)	**teu**	Teoo	**tua**	TOOa
his, her, its, your (polite)	**seu**	SEoo	**sua**	SOOa
your (plural familiar)	**vosso**	VOSsoo	**vossa**	VOSsa
our	**nosso**	NOSsoo	**nossa**	NOSsa
their, your (plural polite)	**seu**	SEoo	**sua**	SOOa

The other thing to note is that the article 'the' is used before possessives. Remember that it changes according to the gender of the noun it precedes.

Plural possessives are formed just by adding s.

Here are some examples now containing all the above information:

A minha filha 'my daughter'; **o seu chapéu** 'his, her, your hat'; **os nossos livros** 'our books'

Note: The seeming confusion of **seu** meaning so many things does not arise when in context. In Brazilian Portuguese, however, there is a different way of expressing 'his, her' etc. See the section on Brazilian Portuguese after this Grammar Guide.

Verbs

We shall give all the persons in the verb tables, but in fact throughout this phrase-book we have only used the polite form of 'you', '**você**'. ('**Tu**' is used for friends, family and children.) **Você** is followed by the form of the third person singular, as he, she and it.

However, in Portuguese the personal pronoun, *e.g.* I, you, he etc., is often left out; the important part of the verb therefore is the ending. (It is only where there might be ambiguity that you use the pronoun.)

E.g. **Como está?** How are you?

Note: The phonetic equivalent of the most common forms of these verbs is given throughout the phrase book, so here we are giving just the grammatical forms. There are two verbs in Portuguese meaning '*to be*': **ser** and **estar**. Here are the basic differences between the usages of the two verbs:

ser is used to refer to a permanent, unchanging state or fact, such as in 'He is English' '**É inglês**'.

Estar is used when referring to a temporary condition or activity, such as in **Estou cansado** (I'm tired) and **Estou a estudar** (I'm studying).

		Ser	Estar
Eu	(I)	sou	estou
Tu	(You) (familiar)	és	estás
Ele/ela	(He/she/it)	é	está
Voce	(You) (polite)		
Nos	(We)	somos	estamos
Vos	(You) (fam. plural)	sois	estais
Eles	(They)	são	estão

Note: To express 'there is/there are' the Portuguese say **há**. . . .

To have is expressed by the verb **ter**.

Eu	tenho
Tu	tens
Ele/ela Você }	tem
Nos	temos
Vos	tendes
Eles/vocês	têm

The following three verbs are indispensable to any traveller anywhere: 'can', 'want' and 'must', namely **poder**, **querer** and the verb-phrase **ter de**:

	poder (can)	querer (want)
Eu	posso	quero
Tu	podes	queres
Ele/ela Você }	pode	quer
Nos	podemos	queremos
Vos	podeis	quereis
Eles/vocês	podem	querem

You have already seen the verb **ter**. To express 'must' you simply add **de** and then the infinitive, *e.g.* **tenho de pagar** (I must pay).

Examples of the other two verbs above: **quero fumar** (I want to smoke) and **posso ajudar** (I can help).

Negatives
To express the negative of any verb simply put **não** in front of it, *e.g.* **não fumo** (I don't smoke), **não quero** (I don't want (to)).

Questions
Questions are formed just by raising the tone of one's voice questioningly at the end of the sentence, *e.g.* **Fuma?** (Do you smoke?)

Most main verbs nearly all follow one of the three forms below:

Verbs ending in:

-ar	-er	-ir
1. falar 'to speak'	2. **vender** 'to sell'	3. **partir** 'to leave'
Eu falo	vendo	parto
Tu falas	vendes	partes
Ele/ela ⎫ Você ⎭ fala	vende	parte
Nos falamos	vendemos	partimos
Vos falais	vendeis	partis
Eles/vocês falam	vendem	partem

Two very useful irregular verbs are **ir** (to go) and **dizer** (to say):

	Ir (to go)	Dizer (to say)
Eu	vou	digo
Tu	vais	dizes
Ele/ela ⎫ Você ⎭	vai	diz
Nos	vamos	dizemos
Vos	ides	dizeis
Eles/vocês	vão	dizem

Comparatives and superlatives

These are quite simple. The comparative is formed by putting the word **mais** before the adjective and **do que** after it,

> *E.g.* **Maria é mais bonita do que Gabriela**
> (Maria is prettier than Gabriela)

To express 'less' substitute **menos** for **mais**,

> *E.g.* **Luisa é menos alta do que Inês**
> (Luisa is less tall than Ines)

The superlative is formed by putting **o** or **a** before **mais** (depending on the gender of the noun being described) and **de** afterwards,

> *E.g.* **João é o mais alto de todos**
> (John is the tallest of all)

Some useful exceptions:

bom	(good)	**melhor**	(better)
mau	(bad)	**pior**	(worse)
grande	(big)	**maior**	(bigger)
pequeno	(small)	**menor**	(smaller)

o/a **melhor** de ...	(the best ...)
o/a **pior** de ...	(the worst ...)
o/a **maior** de ...	(the biggest ...)
o/a **mais pequeno** de ...	(the smallest ...)

Don't forget the **de** in these phrases contracts when it's next to **o/a** (the) or **um/uma** (a(n)), *e.g.* to **do/da** or **dum/duma**.

The Differences between Brazilian and European Portuguese

Pronunciation

The sounds are basically the same in Brazilian as in European Portuguese, but as the Brazilians speak the language more slowly, every syllable is more clearly pronounced. It is, in fact, easier for English people to understand as the vowels are less 'swallowed' and so the words sound more like the way they appear on the printed page.

There are three sounds which *are* pronounced differently. One is the final 'e' and the others, especially round Rio de Janeiro, are the 'd' and the 't' before the final 'e'.

Instead of being silent or barely heard, as in European Portuguese, the Brazilian final 'e' is pronounced ee. The 'd' before it sounds like our 'j' as in jug and the 't' before it sounds like 'ch' as in chair.

So, in Brazilian Portuguese:

> **de** is pronounced jee
> **tarde** is pronounced TARjee
> **onde** is pronounced ONjee
> **quente** is pronounced KENchee
> **frente** is pronounced FRENchee
> **telefone** is pronounced teləFONee

The circumflex accent (*e.g.* ô) oh is used more in Brazilian than in European Portuguese.

S or **z** at the end of a word is pronounced more as s or z and not sh as in Portuguese.

Grammar

There are also only a few significant differences in this area of the language:

Verb forms

You will notice throughout this book that when you want to ask someone to do something for you, you say **'Pode-me . . .'** POD-mə (Could you . . .). In Brazilian Portuguese this is reversed and you say **'Me pode . . .'** mə POjee. . . .

When describing what you are in the process of doing, in European Portuguese you use the form: **stou a** + infinitive (**stou a fazer**),

E.g. **Stou a estudar**   shtoh a shtooDAR (I'm studying).

In Brazilian Portuguese you must use the form **estou** + Gerund (*i.e.* the equivalent of our '—ing' form in I'm studying) (**estou fazendo**).

E.g. **estou estudando**   shtoh shtooDANdoo.

The verb **'ir'** (to go) is followed by different prepositions in the two languages.

In European Portuguese it is followed by **'a'** or **'para'**. *E.g.* **vou a/para Portugal**   (I'm going to Portugal), **vou para a casa de João**   (I'm going to John's house).

In Brazilian Portuguese it is followed by **'em'** and its various forms when before an article. *E.g.* **vou no Portugal**   (I'm going to Portugal), **vou na casa de João**   (I'm going to John's house).

To express 'you', the Brazilians use **'você'** all the time. This again is easier for English people as it means you do not have to worry about whether to call people by the familiar **'tu'** form or the more formal (in European Portuguese) **você**.

Possessives

When saying 'his' or 'her' the Brazilians avoid the ambiguity of the European Portuguese **'seu'** (which can also mean 'your', corresponding with **'você'**). They do this by saying literally 'the book of him/her'. *E.g.* European Portuguese **'o seu livro'** (his/her/your book) becomes in Brazilian Portuguese **'o livro dêle'** (his book), **'o livro dela'** (her book), **'o livro de você'** (your book).

Vocabulary

As in American English and English, there are a few words which either have totally different meanings or which just do not exist in either Brazilian or European Portuguese.

If you know some Portuguese and plan to go to Brazil, or vice versa, you must learn the following words. Otherwise you will either be misunderstood or be laughed at for making a *faux pas*!

European Portuguese	Brazilian Portuguese	English
Greetings		
Como está? KOmoo shta	**Como vai?** KOmoo vy	How are you?
Adeus aDEoosh	**Até logo** aTAY LOgoo	Goodbye
Travelling		
bilheteira beelyəTAYra	**guichet** geeSHAY	ticket office
autocarro owtooKAhoo	**ônibus** OHneeboos	bus
eléctrico eeLEKtreekoo	**bonde** BONjee	tram
comboio komBOIoo	**trem** trayng	train
Police		
polícia pooLEESya	**policial** pooleesYAL	policeman
esquadra SHKWAdra	**delegacia** deləgaSEEa	police station

European Portuguese	Brazilian Portuguese	English
At the hotel/restaurant		
pequeno almoço peKAYnoo alMOsoo	**café da manhã** kaFAY da manYÃ	breakfast
casa de banho KAza də BANyoo	**banheiro** banYAIRoo	lavatory
criado/empregado kreeAdoo/eemprəGAdoo	**garçon** garSONG	waiter
Telephoning		
ligar leeGAR	**discar** deeshKAR	to dial six
seis saysh	**meia** MAYa	(when saying a phone number etc.)
Clothes		
casaco kaZAkoo	**paletó** paləTOH	jacket
camisa de noite kaMEEza də noit	**camisola de noite** kameeZOla də noit	nightdress
camisola kameeZOla	**sweater** SWETair	sweater
fato de banho FAtoo də BANyoo	**maiô** myOH	swimming costume
fato FAtoo	**terno** TAIRnoo	suit
carteira karTAYra	**bolsa** BOLsa	handbag
Colours		
cinzento seenZENtoo	**cinzo** SEENzoo	grey
castanho kashTANyoo	**marron** maHON	brown
Verbs		
perceber pərsəBAIR	**entender** eentənDAIR	to understand
guiar geeAR **conduzir** kondooZEER	**dirigir** deereeZHEER	to drive
por pohr	**botar** booTAR	to put

European Portuguese	Brazilian Portuguese	English
Miscellaneous		
rapariga rapaREEga	**moça** MOssa	girl
bicha BEEsha	**fila** FEEla	queue
constipação konshteepaSOWNG	**resfriado** rəzfreeAdoo	a cold
relva RELva	**grama** GRAma	grass/lawn
fumo FOOmoo	**fumaça** fooMAsa	smoke

Money

The name of the currency unit in Portugal is **escudo**/SHKOOdoo. In Brazil it is **cruzeiro**/krooZAYroo. Both are divided into 100 **centavos** (senTAvoosh).

Cultural differences

Perhaps we can again draw a comparison between Britain and the United States when talking about Portugal and Brazil. The general attitude to life seems more easy-going, the people seem more out-going and friendly. There is less formality in Brazil than in Portugal.

There is one thing to remember in Brazil, however, which does not apply in Portugal, and that is that if you want anyone to do anything for you, you will have to give something more financially rewarding than mere gratitude!

This does not mean that you don't tip. 10 to 15% is expected for any service.

Food

For specific Brazilian dishes, see the end of the Menu section under 'Restaurants, Cafés and Bars'.

Everyday Words and Phrases

Everyday words

Here are some useful adjectives and adverbs and their opposites;
the more of them you get to know by heart, the more easily you
will find you can communicate.

good	**bom**	bong
bad	**mau**	MAoo
better	**melhor**	məlYOR
worse	**pior**	pYOR
cheap	**barato**	baRAtoo
expensive	**caro**	KAroo
right	**correcto**	kooHEToo
wrong	**incorrecto**	eenkooHEToo
big	**grande**	grand
small	**pequeno**	peKAYnoo
hot	**quente**	kent
cold	**frio**	FREEoo
near	**perto**	PAIRtoo
far	**longe**	lonzh
early	**cedo**	SEdoo
late	**tarde**	tard
next	**próximo**	PROSseemoo
last	**último**	OOLteemoo
open	**aberto**	aBAIRtoo
closed	**fechado**	feSHAdoo
vacant	**livre**	LEEvrə
occupied	**ocupado**	okooPAdoo
easy	**fácil**	FAseel
difficult	**difícil**	deeFEEseel
quick	**depressa**	dePRESsa
slow	**devagar**	dəvaGAR
full	**cheio**	SHAYoo

empty	**vazio** vaZEEoo
heavy	**pesado** peZAdoo
light	**leve** lev
beautiful	**bonito** booNEEtoo
ugly	**feio** FAYoo
old	**velho** VELyoo
young	**jovem** ZHOvayng
new	**novo** NOvoo
clever	**esperto** SHPAIRtoo
stupid	**estupido** SHTOOpeedoo
ill	**doente** dwent
well	**bem** bayng

A few words which can be used with the preceding adjectives and adverbs:

very	**muito** MWEENtoo
too	**demasiado** dəmazYAdoo
enough	**bastante** bashTANT
a little	**um pouco** oong POHkoo

Also **mais** (more) and **menos** (less) in the comparative and superlative (see the end of the Basic Grammar Guide).

Lastly, a list of words necessary for most sentences, but especially useful for directions and instructions:

and	e ee
in	**em** ayng
to	**para/a** PAra/a
at	**em** ayng
on	**sobre** SOBrə
from	**de** də
of	**de** də
with	**com** kong
without	**sem** sayng
for	**por/para** poor/PAra
near	**perto** PAIRtoo

past (beyond)	além	aLAYNG
next to	ao lado de	Aoo LAdoo də
behind	atrás	aTRASH
in front of	em frente	ayng frent
opposite	oposto	ooPOSHtoo
(a)round	em volta	ayng VOLta
over	por cima	poor SEEma
above	em cima	ayng SEEma
before (time)	antes de	ANTəsh də
after (time)	depois de	dəPOISH də
after (place)	a seguir	a səGEER
under	debaixo de, sob	dəBYshoo də/sob
through	através	atraVAYSH

E.g. **Hoje estou em casa.**　ozh shtoh ayng KAza
(Today I'm at home.)

Amanhã vou para Italia.　amanYÃ voh PAra
(Tomorrow I'm going to Italy.)　eeTALya

Vou com uns amigos.　voh kong oongsh
(I'm going with friends.)　aMEEgoosh

Useful phrases

Greetings

Good morning.	**Bom dia.** bong DEEa
Good afternoon.	**Boa tarde.** BOHa tard
Good evening.	**Boa noite.** BOHa noit
Good night.	**Boa noite.** BOHa noit
Goodbye.	**Adeus.** aDAYoosh
See you. . . .	**Até. . . .** aTAY

–this evening.	**logo à noite.**
	LOgoo a noit
–tomorrow.	**amanhã.**
	amanYÃ
–this afternoon.	**logo à tarde.**
	LOgoo a tard
–later.	**logo.**
	LOgoo

Anywhere

Yes.	**Sim.**
	seeng
No.	**Não.**
	nowng
Thank you.	**Obrigado.**
	obreeGAdoo
Thank you very much.	**Muito obrigado.**
	MWEENtoo obreeGAdoo
Please.	**Por favor/faz favor.**
	poor faVOOR/fazh faVOOR
Of course/surely.	**Com certeza.**
	kong sərTEza
Excuse me, may I . . .?	**Faz favor, posso . . .?**
	fazh faVOOR, POSsoo
It's very kind of you.	**É muito amável.**
	ay MWEENtoo aMAvel
What did you say?	**Como?**
	KOmoo
Sorry.	**Desculpe.**
	dəshhKOOP
I'm very sorry.	**Sinto muito.**
	SEENtoo MWEENtoo
I beg your pardon.	**Perdão.**
	pərDOWNG
That's all right.	**Está bem.**
	shta bayng

Never mind.   **Não importa.**
                                       nowng eemPORT

Note: We have given two phrases for 'please': **por favor** is simply more formal than **faz favor**.

Language problems

I don't understand.	**Não percebo.** nowng pərSEboo
Do you speak English?	**Fala Inglês?** FAla eenGLAYSH
I don't speak Portuguese.	**Eu não falo Português.** Eoo nowng FAloo portooGAYSH
Does anyone here speak English?	**Alguem aqui fala Inglês?** alGAYNG aKEE FAla eenGLAYSH
Please speak more slowly.	**Faz favor fale mais devagar.** fazh faVOOR fal mysh dəvaGAR
What does . . . mean?	**O que quer . . . dizer?** oo kee kair . . . deeZAIR
Could you translate this, please?	**Pode-me traduzir isto, faz favor?** POD-mə tradooZEER EESHtoo fazh faVOOR
Yes, I understand.	**Sim, percebo.** seeng pərSEboo

Questions

Where is . . . ?	**Onde é . . . ?** ONDee ay . . .
Where are . . . ?	**Onde são . . . ?** ONDee sowng . . .
What time is it?	**Que horas são?** kee Orash sowng

What is this?	**O que é isto?**
	oo kee ay EESHtoo
When is . . .?	**Quando é . . .?**
	KWANdoo ay
How much is . . .?	**Quanto custa . . .?**
	KWANtoo KOOSHta
How far is . . .?	**Qual é a distancia até . . .?**
	kwal ay a deeshTANSya aTAY
How long does . . . take?	**Quanto tempo leva . . .?**
	KWANtoo TEMpoo LEVa
How?	**Como?**
	KOmoo
Who?	**Quem?**
	kayng
Why?	**Porquê?**
	poorKAY
Why not?	**Porque não?**
	POORkə nowng
What do you want?	**O que é que quere?**
	oo kee ay kə kair
What's the matter?	**O que aconteceu?**
	oo kee akontəSEoo

All the necessary questions will be given in full in all the situations where they might occur.

Meeting people

How do you do?	**Muito prazer.**
	MWEENtoo prəZAIR
I'm pleased to meet you.	**Tenho muito gosto em o conhecer.**
	TENyoo MWEENtoo GOSHtoo ayng oo konyəSAIR
How are you?	**Como está?**
	KOmoo shta

Very well thank you.	**Muito bem obrigado.**
	MWEENtoo bayng obreeGAdoo

When you introduce somebody it is only necessary to say their name.

Mr. . . .	**–O senhor. . . .**
	–oo sənYOR
Mrs. . . .	**–A senhora. . . .**
	–a sənYORa
my husband.	**–O meu marido.**
	–oo MEoo maREdoo
my wife.	**–A minha mulher.**
	–a MEENya moolYAIR
my friend .	**–O meu amigo.**
	–oo MEoo aMEEgoo
my boy-friend.	**–O meu amigo.**
	–oo MEoo aMEEgoo
my girl-friend.	**–A minha amiga.**
	–a MEENya aMEEga
How is . . .?	**Como está . . .?**
	KOmoo shta

Small talk

Here are a few phrases and questions to help you meet and talk to people on a social level.

Hello.	**Olá.**
	o-LA
What's your name?	**Como se chama?**
	KOmoo sə SHAmə
I'm English.	**Eu sou inglês.**
	Eoo soh eenGLAYSH
Where do you come from?	**Donde é que você é?**
	DONdee ay kə voSAY ay

Do you like it here?	**Gosta de cá estar?** GOSHta də ka shtar
I like . . .	**Eu gosto de . . .** Eoo GOSHtoo də
I don't like . . .	**Eu não gosto de . . .** Eoo nowng GOSHtoo də
Have you got a light, please?	**Tem lume, faz favor?** tayng loom fazh faVOOR
Do you smoke?	**Fuma?** FOOma
Would you like . . .	**Quer . . .** kair
–a drink?	**–tomar uma bebida?** –toMAR OOma bəBEEda
–a cigarette?	**–um cigarro?** –oong seeGAhoo
–a coffee?	**–tomar um café?** –toMAR oong kaFAY
–to dance?	**–dançar?** –danSAR
–to go out tonight?	**–sair esta noite?** –saEER ESHta noit
–to go to the discothèque?	**–ir a uma discoteca?** –eer a OOma deeshkoTEka
I'm hungry.	**Tenho fome.** TENyoo FOmə
I'm thirsty.	**Tenho sede.** TENyoo sed
I'm tired.	**Estou cansado.** shtoh kənSAdoo
Yes, please.	**Sim, faz favor.** seeng fazh faVOOR
No, thank you.	**Não, obrigado.** nowng obreeGAdoo
Can we meet again?	**Podemo-nos encontrar outra vez?** pooDEmoo-noosh eenkonTRAR OHtra vaysh

When?	**Quando?** KWANdoo
See you again soon.	**Até breve.** aTAY brev
Hope to see you again soon.	**Até breve, espero.** aTAY brev əshPAIRoo
What a pity.	**Que pena.** kə PAYna
Tomorrow....	**Amanhã....** əmanYÃ
–morning.	**–de manhã.** –də manYÃ
–afternoon	**–à tarde.** –a tard
–evening.	**–à noite.** –a noit
Goodbye.	**Adeus.** aDAYoosh

The weather

What's the weather going to be like?	**Como vai estar o tempo?** KOmoo vy shtar oo TEMpoo
–today?	**–hoje?** –ozh
–tomorrow?	**–amanhã?** –amanYÃ
–this afternoon?	**–esta tarde?** –ESHta tard
Is it going to rain?	**Vai chover?** vy shooVAIR
Is it going to be fine?	**Vai estar bom?** vy shtar bong
Is it going to snow?	**Vai nevar?** vy nəVAR

How long is this weather going to last?	**Quanto durará este tempo?**
	KWANtoo dooraRA ESHtə TEMpoo
Is it going to get hotter/colder?	**Vai estar mais calor/frio?**
	vy shtar mysh kaLOR/FREEoo
Is the weather going to change?	**O tempo vai mudar?**
	oo TEMpoo vy mooDAR
It's . . . today, isn't it?	**Hoje faz . . ., nao faz**
	ozh fazh . . . nowng fazh
–cold	**–frio**
	–FREEoo
–hot	**–calor**
	–kaLOOR
It's a lovely day	**Está um dia lindo.**
	shta oong DEEa LEENdoo
What terrible weather.	**Que tempo horrível.**
	kə TEMpoo oHEEvel
What lovely weather.	**Que tempo formidável.**
	kə TEMpoo foormeeDAvel

Questions you may be asked and the answers you may need:

Customs and passport control

*Have you anything to declare?	**Tem alguma coisa a declarar?** tayng alGOOma KOIza a deklaRAR
No, nothing.	**Não, nada.** nowng NAda
Yes.	**Sim, tenho.** seeng TENyoo
*How much money do you have with you?	**Quanto dinheiro tem consigo?** KWANtoo deenYAIRoo tayng konSEEgoo
*How long do you intend to stay?	**Quanto tempo pensa ficar?** KWANtoo TEMpoo PENsa feeKAR
*Where is your visa?	**Onde está o seu visto?** ONDee shta oo SEoo VEESHtoo

How to get to where you're staying

Where is the luggage from flight number . . .?	**Onde está a bagagem do vôo . . .?** ONDee shta a baGAzhem doo voh
My bags aren't here.	**As minhas malas não estão aqui.** ash MEENyash MALash nowng shtowng aKEE
Where is the bureau de change?	**Onde é a casa de câmbio?** ONDee ay a KAza də KAMbyoo
Please change this into. . . .	**Faz favor troque-me isto em. . . .** fazh faVOOR TROKə-mə EESHtoo ayng

Where can I hire a car?	**Onde posso alugar um carro?**
	ONDə POSsoo alooGAR oong KAhoo
Where is the bus to the town centre?	**Onde é o autocarro para o centro?**
	ONDee ay oo AootoKAhoo PAra oo SENtroo
Where can I get a taxi?	**Onde posso apanhar um taxi?**
	ONDə POSsoo apanYAR oong TAKsee
Please take me to Hotel Sunshine.	**Faz favor leve-me ao Hotel Sunshine.**
	fazh faVOOR lev-mə Aoo oTEL Sunshine
How much is it?	**Quanto é?**
	KWANtoo ay
Where do I get the . . . to . . .?	**Aonde posso apanhar o . . . para . . .?**
	aONDə POSsoo apanYAR oo . . . PAra
–underground	**–metropolitano**
	–metroopoleeTAnoo
–train	**–comboio**
	–komBOIoo
–bus	**–autocarro**
	–owtooKAhoo
–tram	**–eléctrico**
	–eeLEKtreekoo
*The . . . is over there.	**A . . . está alí.**
	a . . . shta əLEE
–underground station	**–estação do metropolitano**
	–shtaSOWNG doo metroopoleeTAnoo
–station	**–estação**
	–shtaSOWNG
–bus stop	**–paragem do autocarro**
	–paRAzhayng doo owtooKAhoo

–tram stop	**–paragem do eléctrico**
	–paRAzhayng doo eeLEKtreekoo
–taxi-rank	**–praça dos taxis**
	–PRAsa doosh TAKseesh
When's the next bus/train to . . . ?	**Quando é o próximo autocarro/ comboio para . . . ?**
	KWANdoo ay oo PROSseemoo owtooKAhoo/ komBOIoo PAra

At the Hotel

It is advisable to select your hotel from the hotel guide published by the Portuguese National Tourist Office. This is obtainable from their offices at New Bond St. House, 1 New Bond Street, London, W1. It is also advisable to book in advance in high season. If you can't find a hotel room, go to the local 'turismo' (tourist information office) and they should be able to help you. There is one in most towns.

There are various categories of hotels, from the state-owned **pousadas**, where the prices are controlled and the service and food are excellent, to the **pensão**, which is more like a boarding-house. Here you can get full board or just bed and breakfast. Motels (bed and breakfast) are becoming increasingly popular in Brazil.

Checking in

*Good morning.	**Bom dia.** bong DEEa
*Good afternoon.	**Boa tarde.** BOHa tard
*Good evening.	**Boa noite.** BOHa noit
*Can I help you?	**Posso ajudá-lo?** POSsoo azhooDA-loo
*What's your name?	**Como se chama?** KOMoo sə SHAma
My name is. . . .	**Chamo-me. . . .** SHAmoo-mə
I have a reservation.	**Tenho uma reserva.** TENyoo OOma rəZAIRva
I haven't got a reservation.	**Não tenho reserva.** nowng TENyoo rəZAIRva

*How long are you going to stay?	**Quanto tempo vai ficar?** KWANtoo TEMpoo vy feeKAR
*Please fill in this form.	**Faz favor preencha este impresso.** fazh faVOOR preeENSHa ESHtə eemPRESsoo
*Please give me your passport.	**Dá-me o seu passaporte faz favor.** DAmə oo SEoo pasaPORT fazh faVOOR
I want to stay for. . . .	**Eu quero ficar por. . . .** Eoo KAIRoo feeKAR poor
Have you any vacancies?	**Tem alguma vaga?** tayng alGOOma VAga
Have you a single room?	**Tem um quarto simples?** tayng oong KWARtoo SEEMpləsh
Have you a double room?	**Tem um quarto de casal?** tayng oong KWARtoo də kaZAL
With a bath.	**Com casa de banho.** kong KAza də BANyoo
Without a bath.	**sem casa de banho.** sayng KAza də BANyoo
With a shower.	**com chuveiro.** kong shooVAYroo
Have you half board?	**Tem meia pensão?** tayng MAYa penSOWNG
–full board?	**–pensão completa?** –penSOWNG komPLEtaa
–just bed and breakfast?	**(só) quarto e pequeno almoço?** –(soh) KWARtoo peKAYnoo alMOsoo
Can I have a room . . .?	**Posso ter um quarto . . .?** POSsoo tair oong KWARtoo
–with a double bed?	**–com uma cama de casal?** –kong OOma KAma də kaZAL
–with twin beds?	**–com duas camas?** –kong DOOash KAmash

–with a view of the sea? –com vista para o mar?
kong VEESHta para oo mar

–with a wash-basin? –com um lavatório?
–kong oong lavaTORYoo

–on the ground floor? –no rés-do-chão?
–noo raysh-doo-SHOWNG

–on the first floor? –no primeiro andar?
–noo preeMAYroo anDAR

–on the second floor? –no segundo andar?
–noo səGOONdoo anDAR

Can I see the room first, please? Posso ver o quarto primeiro, por favor?
POSsoo vair oo KWARtoo preeMAYroo fazh faVOOR

Can we have a cot for the child/baby? Pode dar-nos uma cama para a criança/bébé?
pod DARnoosh OOma KAma PAra a kreeANSa/beBAY

Do we pay extra for it? Temos que pagar extra por isso?
TEMoosh kə paGAR AYSHtra poor EESsoo

How much does it cost. . . . Quanto custa. . . .
KWANtoo KOOSHta

–per night? –por noite?
–poor noit

–per week? –por semana?
–poor səMAna

Yes, I'll take the room. Sim, quero o quarto.
seeng, KAIRoo oo KWARtoo

No, I won't take it. Não, não o quero.
nowng, nowng oo KAIRoo

It's too small. É muito pequeno.
ay MWEENtoo peKAYnoo

It's too dark. É muito escuro.
ay MWEENtoo shKOOroo

General

Where is. . . .	**Onde é. . . .**
	ONDee ay
–the car-park?	**–o parque de estacionamento?**
	–oo park də shtasyonaMENtoo
–the lift?	**–o elevador?**
	–oo eləvəDOR
–the dining-room?	**–a casa de jantar?**
	–a KAza də zhanTAR
–the bar?	**–o bar?**
	–oo bar
–the lavatory?	**–a casa de banho?**
	a KAza de BANyoo
–the bathroom?	**–a casa de banho?**
	–a KAza də BANyoo
–the lounge?	**–a sala?**
	–a SAla
–the hairdresser?	**–o cabeleireiro?**
	–oo kabələRAYroo
What time is. . . .	**À que horas é. . . .**
	a kee Orash ay
–breakfast?	**–o pequeno almoço?**
	–oo peKAYnoo alMOsoo
–lunch?	**–o almoço?**
	–oo alMOsoo
–dinner?	**–o jantar?**
	–oo zhanTAR
Room service, please.	**Serviço de Quarto, faz favor.**
	SairVEEsoo de KWARtoo fazh faVOOR
Can I have . . . in my room, please?	**Posso tomar. . . no meu quarto, faz favor?**
	POSsoo toMAR . . . noo MEoo KWARtoo fazh faVOOR
–breakfast	**–o pequeno almoço**
	oo peKAYnoo alMOsoo

–coffee	**–café**
	–kaFAY
–tea	**–chá**
	–sha

At the reception desk

Can I have my key, please?	**A minha chave, faz favor?**
	a MEENya shav fazh faVOOR
I've lost my key.	**Perdi a minha chave.**
	pairDEE a MEENya shav
Please call me at . . . tomorrow.	**faz favor acorde-me às . . . amanhã.**
	fazh faVOOR aKORdə mə ash . . . amanYÃ
Are there any letters for me?	**Há alguma carta para mim?**
	a alGOOma KATta PAra meeng
–messages	**–algum recado**
	–alGOONG reKAdoo
The light doesn't work.	**A luz não acende.**
	a loosh nowng aSEND
The air-conditioning doesn't work.	**O ar condicionado não funciona**
	oo ar kondeesyoNAdoo nowng foonsYOna
The razor socket doesn't work.	**A tomada da máquina de barbear não funciona**
	a tooMAda də barbeAR
The heating doesn't work.	**O aquecimento não funciona**
	oo akeseeMENtoo
The radio doesn't work.	**O rádio não funciona**
	oo RADyoo
The lock doesn't work.	**A fechadura não funciona**
	a feshaDOOra
There's no hot water.	**Não há água quente.**
	nowng a-AGwa kent
–electricity	**–electricidade.**
	–lektreeseeDAD

When someone knocks at the door

Come in.	**Entre.**
	ENtra
Please wait a moment.	**Espere um momento por favor.**
	SHPAIR oong moMENtoo fazh faVOOR
Please come back later.	**Volte mais tarde por favor.**
	VOLt mysh tard fazh faVOOR

If you need something

Please bring me. . . .	**Faz favor traga-me. . . .**
	fazh faVOOR TRAgə-mə
–a towel.	**–uma toalha.**
	–OOma toALya
–a blanket.	**–um cobertor.**
	–oong koobairTOOR
–a pillow.	**–uma almofada.**
	–OOma almoFAda
–an ashtray.	**–um cinzeiro.**
	–oong seengZAYroo
–some coathangers.	**–uns cabides.**
	–oongsh kaBEEdəsh
–some soap.	**–um sabonete.**
	–oong saboNET
–a needle and cotton.	**–una agulha e linha.**
	–OOma aGOOLya ee LEENya
I'd like Room Service, please.	**Ligue-me ao Servico de Quarto faz favor.**
	LEEgə-mə owng SairVEEsoo de KWARtoo fazh faVOOR

At reception on leaving

Please give me the bill.	**A conta por favor.**
	a KONta poor faVOOR
What's this entry on the bill?	**O que é esta entrada na conta?**
	oo kee ay ESHtə eenTRAda na KONta

Is service included in the total?

O servico está incluído no total?
oo sairVEEsoo shta
    eenklooEEdoo noo toTAL

Can I have a receipt?

Pode-me dar um recibo?
POD-mə dar oong rəSEEboo

Here is my home address.

Aqui tem a minha morada.
aKEE tayng a MEENya
    moRAda

Here is my forwarding address.

**Aqui tem a morada para o envio
da minha correspondência.**
aKEE tayng a moRAda PAra
    oo eenVEEoo da MEENya
    kohesponDENSya

I'm leaving this afternoon/
tomorrow.

**Eu saio do hotel esta tarde/
amanhã.**
Eoo SYoo doo oTEL ESHtə
    tard/amanYÃ

Could you order a taxi for . . .
o'clock?

**Pode-me chamar um taxi para as
. . . horas?**
POD-mə shaMAR oong TAKsee
    PAra ash . . . Orash

Please could someone bring my
bags down?

**Por favor, alguém pode trazer as
minhas malas para baixo?**
poor faVOOR alGAYNG pod
    traZAIR ash MEENyash
    MALash PAra BYshoo

Camping and Caravanning

A list of camp-sites (**parques de campismo**) is obtainable from the Portuguese National Tourist Office, New Bond Street House, 1 New Bond Street, London, W1. These offer very reasonable prices and amenities.

At the time of printing, International Camping Cards were not required to enter any camp-site.

If you are taking your caravan to Portugal, you will need to take the log-book, Green Card and an inventory for the Customs.

Where's the nearest. . . .	**Onde é o . . . mais perto?** ONDee ay oo . . . mysh PAIRtoo
–camp site?	**–parque de campísmo?** –park də kamPEEZHmoo
–caravan site?	**–parque de campísmo?** –park də kamPEEZHmoo
–youth hostel?	**–albergue de juventude?** –alBAIRG də zhoovənTOOD
How much is it. . . .	**Quanto custa. . . .** KWANtoo KOOSHta
–per night?	**–por noite?** –poor noit
–per week?	**–por semana?** –poor səMAna
Are there. . . .	**Há. . . .** a
–lavatories?	**–casas de banho?** –KAzash də BANyoo
–washing facilities?	**–serviço de água?** –sairVEEsoo də AGwa
–telephones?	**–telefones?** –teləFONSH

Is there. . . .	Há. . . .
	a
–a shop?	–alguma loja?
	–alGOOma lozh
–a launderette?	–alguma lavandaria?
	alGOOma lavandəREEa
–a restaurant?	–algum restaurante?
	–alGOONG rəshtowRANT
–a bar?	–algum bar?
	–alGOONG bar
–a camping supplies shop?	–alguma loja de campísmo?
	–alGOOma lozh də kamPEEZHmoo
How far is it from . . .?	A que distância fica de . . .?
	a kə deeshTANSya FEEka də

VOCABULARY

tent	tenda TENDa
tent-pole	pau da tenda PAoo da TENDa
tent-pegs	espéques shPEKəSH
groundsheet	chão da tenda showng də TENDə
sleeping-bag	saco de dormir SAKoo də doorMEER
camp-bed	cama de campanha KAma də kamPANya
air-mattress	colchão koolSHOWNG
Primus stove	esquentador shkentaDOOR
camping-gas	gás butano gash booTAnoo
gas-light	lâmpada de gás LAMpədə də gash
tool-kit	caixa de ferramentas KYSHə də fehaMENtash
first aid kit	estojo de primeiros socorros shTOZHoo də preeMAYroosh sooKOhoosh
torch	lanterna lanTAIRna
rope	corda KORda
matches	fósforos FOSHfooroosh
tin-opener	abre-latas ABrə-LAtash
bottle-opener	saca-rolhas SAka-ROLyash

USEFUL SIGNS

Sentido proibido	No entry
Trânsito proibido a todos os veículos automóveis	No entry for motor vehicles
Propriedade privada	Private property
Intrusos serão processados	Trespassers will be prosecuted
Trânsito proibido a roulottes/ reboques de campismo	No caravans
Proibido o campismo	Camping forbidden
Água potável	Drinking water
Água não potável	Not drinking water

Youth Hostelling

For the latest information on youth hostels in Portugal, contact the Youth Hostel Association at 29 John Adam Street, London, WC2.

Don't forget to have a current international Youth Hostelling card when you leave for your holiday!

Where's the nearest youth hostel?	**Onde é o albergue de juventude mais perto?**
	ONDee ay oo alBAIRG də zhoovənTOOD mysh PAIRtoo
I'd like to stay here. . . .	**Gostaria de passar aqui. . . .**
	goshtaREEa də pasSAR aKEE
–for one night.	**–uma noite.**
	–OOma noit
–for two nights.	**–duas noites.**
	–DOOash NOITəsh
*I'm afraid we haven't any room.	**Não temos lugar/vagas.**
	nowng TEMoosh looGAR/ VAgash
*Show me your international youth-hostelling card.	**Mostre-me o seu cartão internacional.**
	MOSHtrə-mə oo SEoo karTOWNG eentərnasyoNAL
*You can only stay one night.	**Só pode ficar por uma noite.**
	soh pod feeKAR poor OOma noit
I'd like. . . .	**Queria. . . .**
	keREEa
–a sleeping bag.	**–um saco de dormir.**
	–oong SAKoo də doorMEER
–a blanket.	**–um cobertor.**
	–oong koobairTOOR

–a pillow.	**–uma almofada.** –OOma almoFAda
–a packed lunch	**–um almoco empacotado** –oong alMOsoo ayngpakooTAdoo
–some hot water.	**–água quente.** –AGwa kent
Where's the. . . .	**Onde é. . . .** ONDee ay
–kitchen?	**–a cozinha?** –a koZEENya
–bathroom?	**–a casa de banho?** –a KAza də BANyoo
–shower-room?	**–o chuveiro?** –oo shooVAIRoo
Where are the wash-basins?	**Onde são os lavabos?** ONDee sowng oosh laVAboosh
What time must we be out in the morning?	**A que horas teremos de sair de manhã?** aa kee Orash təREmoosh də saEER də manYÃ
What time can we come in in the evening?	**A que horas poderemos vir à noite?** aa kee Orash podəRAYmoosh veer a noit
What time must we be in at night?	**Até que horas teremos que chegar à noite?** aTAY kee Orash təREmoosh kə sheGAR a noit
Do you give meals here?	**Servem refeições aqui?** sərVAYNG rəfaySOengsh aKEE
Where else can we stay cheaply?	**Que outros sítios há assim baratos?** kee OHtroosh SEETyoosh a sSEENG baRAtoosh
Where is that?	**Onde fica isso?** ONDə FEEka EESsoo
Where can I leave. . .	**Onde posso deixar. . .** ONDə POSsoo daySHAR

-my bags?

-my rucksack?

-my bicycle?

-as minhas malas?
-ash MEENyash MAlash
-a minha mochila
-a MEENya mooSHEEla
-a minha bicicleta
-a MEENya beeseeKLEta

A short guide to the different regions of Portugal

Whether you want to stay on the beach, go touring or visit historically interesting places, Portugal is the ideal place for a holiday.

Having a long and varied coastline it offers great beach holidays, from Viana do Castelo in the Minho province in the north to the perhaps better known Algarve in the south. Thanks to its geographical position the summer temperatures vary hardly at all from north to south; in the summer you can be virtually guaranteed a hot sunny stay wherever you are. And being on the Atlantic, Portugal always has a gentle sea breeze to take the edge off the heat.

A motoring holiday is well worth while. Portugal has such varied scenery and a wealth of historically interesting, beautiful sights. Generally speaking, the north is more mountainous and the south flatter, but a range of mountains runs down the whole eastern side of the country to form a natural boundary with Spain.

The northern provinces of Minho and Douro are lush and very green, the Douro valley being famous for its vineyards which provide Port wine; the name comes from Porto (the Portuguese name for Oporto), the city which stands at the mouth of the river Douro. Oporto, the city of Henry the Navigator, who in the early fifteenth century discovered parts of the world never known before, is well worth a visit.

The capital of Portugal, Lisbon, stands at the mouth of the other great Portuguese river, the Tagus. This river is generally acknowledged to be the dividing line between northern and southern Portugal. Lisbon is the other port from where great explorers such as Vasco de Gama set sail in the fifteenth century on their voyages of discovery.

One can spend at least a week in Lisbon doing nothing but sight-seeing. You must not miss the monastery of Jerónimos, the tower of Belém, the Castelo Saõ Jorge, the coach museum, the Gulbenkian museum, the museum of ancient art and the national art gallery, to name but a few of the sights. There are wonderful walks to be had, both through the old 'bairros' (districts) of the city, with their narrow little alleyways, or on the hills around the city, which afford striking views of some of the monuments. So, go armed with a good map. There is also a publication in English, *What's on in Lisbon*, which gives up-to-the-minute information on forth-coming events, opening times of museums and so on.

Within easy reach of Lisbon are many interesting places such as the old town of Sintra with its eighth-century Moorish palace, and the coastal resorts of the Costa do Sol: Estoril and Caiscais. These two towns, the dignified tourist resort and the old fishing-port turned rival resort are both famous for their sea-food restaurants.

Directly between Oporto and Lisbon is the old city of Coimbra which should not be missed. This quiet picturesque city claims to have the oldest university in Portugal, and is a city full of tradition. It rivals Lisbon for its 'fados', typical folksongs (see the section on Entertainment on page 112).

The Algarve, the southernmost province of Portugal, is like the island of Madeira in that it is like a huge garden. Besides its fantastic beaches it has some interesting towns to visit such as Faro and Lagos.

Portugal is ideal for a camping holiday too: there are camp-sites near all the main cities and resorts. (See the section on Camping and Caravanning.)

Things to buy in Portugal
If you want to bring something home, find out if there is a local pottery or tile factory. Hand-painted dishes and pots are very pretty and of course Portugal has a long tradition of tile-making, dating from the middle of the sixteenth century. The tiles are called 'azulejos'. Embroidery is another Portuguese speciality and also filigree jewellery; and there is always the wine, port or Madeira!

At the mainline station

It is advisable to book in advance for the express trains to Paris or Madrid. Booking and inquiries can be made at a travel agent. There are two classes of seats: first and second.

I'd like a single/return ticket to. . . .	**Queria um bilhete de ida/(de ida e volta) para. . . .** keREEa oong beelYET də EEda/də EEda ee VOLta PAra
*First or second class?	**Primeira ou segunda classe?** preeMAIRa oh səGOONda klas
What's the single/return fare?	**Quanto é o bilhete de ida e volta?** KWANtoo ay oo beelYET də EEda ee VOLta
What's the fare for a child?	**Quanto é o bilhete de criança?** KWANtoo ay oo beelYET də kreeANsa
Can I reserve a seat?	**Posso reservar lugar?** POSsoo rəzərVAR looGAR
I'd like a seat. . . .	**Queria um lugar.** keREEa oong looGAR

–in a smoking compartment	–numa carruagem onde seja permitido fumar.
	–NOOma karoAZHayng ondə SAYzha pərmeeTEEdoo fooMAR
–in a no-smoking compartment.	–numa carruagem onde não seja permitido fumar.
	–NOOma karooAZHayng ondə nowng SAYzha pərmeeTEEdoo fooMAR
–facing the front.	–virado para a frente.
	–veeRAdoo PAra a frent
–with my back to the engine.	–de costas para a locomotiva.
	–də KOSHtash PAra a lokoomooTEEva
Is there. . . .	Há. . . .
	a—
–a buffet-car on the train?	–alguma carruagem bufete no comboio?
	–alGOOma karooAZHayng booFET noo komBOIoo
–a restaurant-car on the train?	–alguma carruagem restaurante no comboio?
	–alGOOMa karooAZHayng rəshtowRANT noo komBOIoo
Is it a sleeper?	E uma carruagem-cama?
	ay OOma karooAZHayng KAma
I'd like to reserve a berth.	Queria reservar um beliche.
	keREEa rəzərVAR oong beLEESH
What time does the train leave?	A que horas parte o combóio?
	a kee Orash part oo komBOIoo
–arrive?	–chega?
	–SHEga
Which platform does it leave from?	De que plataforma parte?
	də kə plataFOORma part

–come in?	–a que plataforma chega? –a kə plataFOORma SHEga
Do I have to change trains?	Tenho que fazer transbordo? TENyoo ke faZAIR transhBOORdoo
Where?	Onde? ONDə
What time is the connection for . . . ?	A que horas se faz a ligação para . . . ? a kee Orash sə fazh a leegaSOWNG PAra
Does this train go to . . . ?	Este comboio vai para . . . ? ESHTə komBOIoo vy PAra
When's the first/last train to . . . ?	Quando é o primeiro/último combóio para . . . ? KWANdoo ay oo preeMAYroo/OOLteemoo komBOIoo PAra
Have you got a timetable, please?	Tem um horário, por favor? tayng oong oRARyoo poor faVOOR
Where is. . . .	Onde é. . . . ONDee ay
–platform X?	–a plataforma X? –a plataFOORma X
–the waiting-room?	–a sala de espera? –a SAla də SHPAIRa
–the bar?	–o bar? –oo bar
–the information office?	–o serviço de informações? –oo sərVEEsoo də eenformaSOengsh

STATION SIGNS

Partidas	Departures
Chegadas	Arrivals
Depósito de bagagem	Left luggage

Plataforma X	Platform X
Perdidos e achados	Lost property
Informações	Information
Bilheteira	Ticket office
Reservas	Reservations
Casa de banho (Senhoras/ **Homens)**	Lavatories (Ladies/Gentlemen)
Casa de banho	Wash-room
Sala de espera	Waiting-room
Bufete	Buffet
Restaurante	Restaurant
Bar	Bar

On the underground

Which line goes to . . .?

Qual é a linha que vai para . . .?
kwal ay a LEENya kə vy PAra

Does this train go to . . .?

Este comboio vai para . . .?
ESHTə komBOIoo vy PAra

Where do I change for . . .?

Aonde é que mudo para . . .?
oONDee ay ke MOOdoo PAra

On the bus

Where do I get a bus to . . .?

Aonde posso apanhar um autocarro para . . .?
aONDee POSsoo apanYAR oong owtooKAhoo PAra

How long does it take?

Quanto tempo leva?
KWANtoo TEMpoo LEva

Do I have to change?

Tenho que mudar?
TENyoo kə mooDAR

Does this bus go to . . .?

Esta autocarro vai para . . .?
ESHta owtooKAhoo vy PAra

How often do they run?	**De quanto em quanto tempo passam?**
	də KWANtoo ayng KWANtoo TEMpoo PASsang
Please tell me when to get off.	**Diga-me quando devo sair, por favor.**
	DEEgə-mə KWANdoo DEvoo sa-EER poor faVOOR
I want to get off at. . . .	**Eu quero sair na. . . .**
	Eoo KAIRoo sa-EER na
Bus stop	**Paragem (do autocarro)**

At the airport

English is the common language at all airports, so you should not normally need to use any phrases in Portuguese.

Which gate for flight number . . .?	**Qual é a porta para o voô . . .?**
	kwal ay a POORta PAra oo voh
My bags aren't here.	**As minhas malas não estão aqui.**
	ash MEENyash MALash nowng shtowng aKEE

Taxis

These are not too pricy and you can ask beforehand what the approximate fare might be. Don't forget to tip at the end of your journey: 10 to 15 per cent of the fare.

I want to go to . . . please.	**Eu quero ir para . . . por favor.**
	Eoo KAIRoo eer PAra . . . poor faVOOR
How much will it cost to go to . . .?	**Quanto é que custa ir a . . .?**
	KWANtoo ay ke KOOSHta eer a
Could you help me with the bags?	**Pode-me ajudar com as malas?**
	POD-mə azhooDAR kong ash MAlash

I'm in a hurry.	**Estou com pressa.**
	shtoh kong PRESsa
Stop here, please.	**Pare aqui, por favor.**
	par aKEE, poor faVOOR
What's the surcharge for?	**Para que é a sobretaxa?**
	PAra kee ay a sohbrəTASHa
Please wait here for me.	**Espere aqui por mim, por favor.**
	shpair aKEE poor meeng poor
	faVOOR

Your car

Documents required if taking your car to Portugal:

A UK Driving Licence; an International Insurance Certificate (Green Card), which must state on the back that it applies to Portugal; your car log book; and GB car plates for the car. For driving in and through Spain, you must have an international driving licence. Either the Automobile Association (Fanum House, Leicester Square, London, WC2) or the Royal Automobile Association (Pall Mall, London, SW1) will be able to give you the latest information and, if necessary, the additional forms for entry and customs formalities.

If you are also taking your caravan, you will need the log book, Green Card and an inventory for the customs.

Driving is on the right in Portugal and at cross-roads priority should be given to cars coming from the right. There are two grades of petrol: 'normal' (2-star) and 'super' (4-star).

Where is . . . ?	**Onde é . . . ?**
	ONDee ay
–the next garage?	**–a próxima garagem?**
	–a PROSseema gaRAzhayng

–the nearest car park?	–o parque de estacionamento mais próximo? oo park də shtasyonaMENtoo mysh PROSseemoo
–the nearest automatic car wash?	–a lavagem automática mais próxima? –a laVAzhayng owtooMAteeka mysh PROSseema
–the motorway?	–a autostrada? –a owtooSHTRAda
Can I park here?	Posso estacionar aqui? POSsoo shtasyoNAR aKEE
What does this sign/notice mean?	O que quer dizer este sinal/aviso? oo kee kair deeZAIR ESHtə seeNAL/aVEEzoo
Excuse me, can you tell me the way to . . .?	Por favor, pode-me indicar o caminho para . . .? poor faVOOR POD-mə eendeeKAR oo kaMEENyoo PAra

(For answers see 'Asking the way & Directions,' page 61.)

At the petrol station

I'd like ten litres of super, please.	Quero dez litros de super, por favor. KAIRoo daysh LEEtroosh də SOOpər poor faVOOR
–normal, please.	–gasolina normal, por favor. –gazoLEEna noorMAL poor faVOOR
Please fill the tank.	Encha por favor. ENsha poor faVOOR
Please check. . . .	Pode ver. . . . POD vair
–the water.	–a água. –a AGwa

–the battery.	**–a bateria.**
	–a batəREEa
–the tyre pressure.	**–a pressão dos pneus.**
	–a preSOWNG doosh PNEoosh
–the oil.	**–o óleo.**
	–oo OHIeoo
Do you sell cigarettes?	**Tem cigarros?**
	tayng seeGAhoosh
–sweets?	**–doces?**
	–DOHsəsh
Where is the lavatory, please?	**Onde é a casa de banho por favor?**
	ONDee ay a KAza də BANyoo poor faVOOR

At the garage for repairs etc.

My car has broken down.	**O meu carro está avariado.**
	oo MEoo KAhoo shta avarYAAdoo
–won't start.	**–não pega.**
	–nowng PEga
I've run out of petrol.	**Faltou-me a gasolina.**
	FALtoh-mə a gazoLEEna
The carburettor is blocked.	**O carburador está entupido.**
	oo karbooraDOOR shta entooPEEdoo
The hand brake isn't working.	**O travão de mão não trava.**
	oo traVOWNG də mowng nowng TRAva
The foot brake. . . .	**O travão de pé. . . .**
	oo traVOWNG də pay
The clutch. . . .	**A embraiagem colou. . . .**
	a eembry-YAzhayng KOloh
The horn. . . .	**A buzina não funciona. . . .**
	a booZEEna nowng foonsyOna
The gears are jammed.	**A caixa de velocidades está presa.**
	a KYSHa də veloseeDADəsh shta PREza

The starter is jammed.	**O motor de arranque está encravado.**
	oo mooTOOR də aHANK shta eenkraVAdoo
The accelerator....	**O acelerado está encravado. ...**
	oo aseləraDOOR shta eenkraVAdoo
The fan-belt is broken.	**Partiu-se a correia da ventoínha.**
	parTEEoo-sə a koHAYa da ventooEENya
The windscreen wipers aren't working.	**Os limpa-pára-brisas ... não trabalham.**
	oosh LEEMpa-PAra-BREEzash nowng traBALyang
The brake lights....	**As luzes do travão. ...**
	ash LOOzəsh doo traVOWNG
The headlights....	**Os faróis da frente. ...**
	oosh faROISH da frent
The indicators....	**O pisca-pisca. ...**
	oo PEESHka-PEESHka
The rear lights....	**As luzes de trás. ...**
	ash LOOzəsh da trash
Could you recharge the battery?	**Pode carregar a bateria?**
	pod kaheGAR a batəREEa
How long will it take to repair?	**Quanto tempo leva o arranjo?**
	KWANtoo TEMpoo LEva oo aHANzhoo
How much will it cost?	**Quanto vai custar?**
	KWANtoo vy kooshTAR
I've got....	**Tenho. ...**
	TENyoo
–a puncture.	**–um pneu furado.**
	–oon PNEoo fooRAdoo
–a flat battery.	**–a bateria descarregada.**
	–a batəREEa dəshkaheGAda
–damp spark-plugs.	**–as velas sujas.**
	–ash VElash SOOzhash

Have you got. . . .	**Tem. . . .**
	tayng
–another tyre?	**–outro pneu?**
	–OHtroo PNEoo
–a can of petrol?	**–uma lata de gasolina?**
	–OOma lata də gazooLEEna
–a can of oil?	**–uma lata de óleo?**
	–OOma LAta də OHleoo
–a can of brake fluid?	**–uma lata de óleo dos travões?**
	–OOma LAta də OHleoo doosh traVOengsh
–a pressure gauge?	**–um manómetro?**
	–oong maNOHmetroo

Hiring a car

I'd like to hire a car, please.	**Queria alugar um carro, por favor.**
	kəREEa alooGAR oong KAhoo poor faVOOR
The smallest/largest you have.	**O carro mais-pequeno/maior que tiver.**
	oo KAhoo mysh peKAYnoo/ myəOR kə teeVAIR
A mini.	**Um mini.**
	oong MEEnee
A saloon.	**Um Automóvel-saloon.**
	oong owtooMOHvel-saLOON
A two-door car.	**Um carro de duas portas.**
	oong KAhoo də DOOash POORtash
A four-door car.	**Um carro de quatro portas.**
	oong KAhoo də KWATroo POORtash

A convertible.	**Um carro descapotável.** oong KAhoo dəshkapoTAvel
With a sun-roof.	**Com um tecto de abrir.** kong oong TETtoo də aBREER
For . . . days.	**Por . . . dias.** poor — DEEash
For one week.	**Por uma semana.** poor OOma səMAna
For two weeks.	**Por duas semanas.** poor DOOash səMAnash
Can I hire a car for one day?	**Posso alugar um carro por um dia?** POSsoo alooGAR oong KAhoo poor oong DEEa
Can I hire a car for the week-end?	**Posso alugar um carro para o fim-de-semana?** POSsoo alooGAR oong KAhoo PAra oo feeng-də-səMAna
Could we have a chauffeur-driven car?	**Podemos ter um carro com motorista/chauffeur?** poDEmoosh tair oong KAhoo kong mootooREEshta/chauffeur
How much does it cost?	**Quanto custa?** KWANtoo KOOSHta
Does that include comprehensive insurance?	**Isso inclui seguro contra todos os ríscos?** EESsoo eenKLOOee səGOOroo KONTra TOHdoosh oosh REESHkoosh
Can I return it in a different town?	**Posso devolver o carro noutra cidade?** POSsoo dəvolVAIR oo KAhoo NOHtra seeDAD

Must I bring it back to this office?	**E preciso devolver o carro a este escritório?** ay prəSEEzoo dəvolVAIR oo KAhoo a ESHtə shkreeTOHryoo
Have you got an office in . . .?	**Têm algum escritório em . . .?** tayng alGOONG shkreeTOHryoo ayng
Is there a deposit?	**E preciso deixar depósito?** ay prəSEEzoo daySHAR dəPOZeetoo
Can I see the car, please?	**Posso ver o carro, por favor?** POSsoo vair oo KAhoo poor faVOOR
I'd like an automatic, please.	**Queria um carro automático, por favor.** kəREEa oong KAhoo owtoMAteekoo poor faVOOR
Can I have a car manual, please?	**Dê-me un livro de instruções para o carro, por favor.** DAY-mə oong LEEvroo də eenshtrooSOengsh PAra oo KAhoo poor faVOOR

WRITTEN ROAD SIGNS

In more rural areas you may still see road-signs written in Portuguese and not the international symbols. Here are some of the more usual ones:

Guie devagar	Drive slowly
Guie com cautela	Drive carefully
Reduza a velocidade	Slow down
Alto/Pare	Halt
Escola	School
Obras	Roadworks
Desvio	Diversion

Autostrada	Motorway
Passagem de nível	Level crossing
Cruzamento	Crossroads
Sentido proibido (rua de sentido único)	No entry (one-way street)
Estacionamento proibido	No parking
Rua privada	Private road
Perigo	Danger

Asking the way and directions

Excuse me.	**Faz favor.**
	fazh faVOOR
Can you tell me the way to . . .?	**Pode-me indicar o caminho para . . .?**
	POD-mə eendeeKAR oo kaMEENyoo PAra
Where is . . .?	**Onde é . . .?**
	ONDee ay
Is it a long walk?	**Há que andar muito?**
	a kee anDAR MWEENtoo
Can I take a bus/train there?	**Posso apanhar algum autocarro/comboio para lá?**
	POSsoo apanYAR alGOONG owtoKAhoo/komBOIoo PAra la
Where am I on this map?	**Onde estou aqui no mapa?**
	ONDee shtoh aKEE noo MApa
Where is it on this map?	**Onde é que isso fica aqui no mapa?**
	ONDee ay kə EESsoo FEEka aKEE noo MApa
*Go back.	**Volte para trás.**
	volt PAra trash

*Carry straight on.	**Continue sempre em frente.**
	konTEEnooə SAYNGprə ayng frent
*Turn right.	**Volte à direita.**
	volt a deeRAYta
*Turn left.	**Volte à esquerda.**
	volt a SHKAIRda
*Take the. . . .	**Volte na. . . .**
	volt na
–first left.	**–primeira à esquerda.**
	–preeMAIRa a SHKAIRda
–second	**–segunda**
	–səGOONda
–third	**–terceira**
	–tərSAIRa
–right/left.	**–à direita/à esquerda.**
	–a deeRAYta/a SHKAIRda
–main road.	**–rua principal.**
	–ROOa preenseePAL
*Cross the road.	**Atravesse a rua.**
	atraVES a ROOa
*At the traffic-lights.	**Nos sinais de trânsito.**
	noosh seeNYeesh də TRANseetoo
*When you reach the cross-roads.	**Ao chegar ao cruzamento.**
	Aoo sheGAR Aoo kroozaMENtoo
*At the cinema.	**Ao chegar ao cinema.**
	Aoo sheGAR Aoo SEEnema
*Then ask again.	**Depois pergunte outra vez.**
	dəPOISH pərGOONT OHtra vesh
*It's right in front of you.	**Fica mesmo em frente.**
	FEEka MEZHmoo ayng frent
*It's only a short way from here.	**É perto de aqui.**
	ay PAIRtoo də aKEE

*It's a long way.

É muito longe.
ay MWEENtoo lonzh

*It's about two blocks from here.

Fica a dois quarteirões de aqui.
FEEka a doish kwartayROengsh
də aKEE

Shopping

In Portugal, opening hours are from 9.00 a.m. to 1.00 p.m. and then from 3.00 to 7.00 p.m. Monday to Friday. Some shops stay open all day Saturday, but most close at lunchtime (1.00 p.m.).

Shops are usually closed on Public Holidays (see list on page 132).

In Brazil, shops are open from 8.00 a.m. to 6.00 p.m. and don't usually close at lunchtime, but they close at noon on Saturdays.

Names of shops and places

baker	**padaria**	padaREEa
bank	**banco**	BANkoo
barber	**barbeiro**	barBAYroo
butcher	**talho**	TALyoo
car park	**parque de estacionamento**	park də shtasyonaMENtoo
chemist	**farmácia**	farMASya
clothes shop	**loja de modas**	LOHzha də MODəsh
electrician	**electricista**	eelektreeSEESHta
florist	**florista**	flooREEshta
grocer	**mercearia**	mərseaREEa
greengrocer	**lugar de hortaliças**	looGAR də oortaLEESash
hairdresser	**cabeleireiro**	kabələRAYroo
ironmonger	**ferreiro**	feHAYroo
laundry	**lavandaria**	lavandaREEa
police station	**esquadra da polícia**	SHKWADra da poLEESya
post office	**correio**	koHAYoo
supermarket	**supermercado**	soopərmərKAdoo
tobacconist	**tabacaria**	tabakaREEa

8

In a food shop

Have you got. . . .	**Tem.** . . . tayng
–butter?	**–manteiga?** –manTAYga
–cheese?	**–queijo?** –KAYzhoo
–milk?	**–leite?** –layt
–cold meats?	**–carnes frias?** –KARNəsh FREEash
–eggs?	**–ovos?** –OHvoosh
Can I have. . . .	**Dá-me.** . . . DA-mə
–a tin of. . . .	**–uma lata de.** . . . –OOma LAta də
–fruit?	**–fruta?** –FROOta
–coffee?	**–café?** –kaFAY
–tomatoes?	**–tomates?** –toMAtəsh
–a packet of. . . .	**–um pacote de.** . . . –oong paKOHT də
–sugar?	**–açúcar?** –aSOOkar
–tea?	**–chá?** –sha
–rice?	**–arroz?** –aHOSH
–a loaf of bread?	**–um pão?** –oong powng
–a bottle of. . . .	**–uma garrafa de.** . . . –OOma gaHAfa də

–milk?	**–leite?**
	–layt
–fruit juice?	**–sumo de fruta?**
	SOOmoo də FROOta
–beer?	**–cerveja?**
	–sərVEzha
–mineral water?	**–água mineral?**
	–AGwa meenəRAL
–soda water?	**–água do Castelo/soda?**
	–AGwa doo kashTEloo/SOHda
–lemonade?	**–limonada?**
	–leemoNAda
Have you got a box, please?	**Arranja-me uma caixa, faz favor?**
	aHANzha-mə OOma KYSHa
	fazh faVOOR
Have you got a carrier bag, please?	**Arranja-me um saco de plástico, faz favor?**
	aHANzha-mə oong SAKoo də
	PLASHteekoo fazh faVOOR

VOCABULARY

Meat and fish

lamb	**carneiro**	karNAIRoo
pork	**porco**	POORkoo
veal	**vitela**	veeTEla
beef	**carne de vaca**	KARN də VAka
steak	**bife**	beef
liver	**fígado**	FEEgadoo
kidneys	**rins**	reengsh
chop	**costeleta**	koshteLEta
ham	**fiambre**	fYAMbrə
sole	**linguado**	leenGWAdoo
tuna	**atum**	aTOONG
red mullet	**tainha vermelha**	ta-EENya vərMELya
sardine	**sardinhas**	sarDEENyash
cod	**bacalhau**	bakalYOW

| turbot | **robalo** rooBAloo |
| trout | **truta** TROOta |

Vegetables and fruit

a kilo of. . . .	**um kilo de. . . .** oong KEEloo də
potatoes	**batatas** baTAtash
tomatoes	**tomates** toMAtəsh
lettuce	**alface** alFAS
carrots	**cenouras** seNOHrash
peas	**ervilhas** ərVEELyash
beans	**feijão** fayZHOWNG
cabbage	**couve** sohv
apples	**maçãs** maSANGSH
oranges	**laranjas** laRANzhash
grapefruit	**toranja** tooRANzha
grapes	**uvas** OOvash
melon	**melão** məLOWNG
bananas	**bananas** baNAnash
peaches	**pêssegos** PAYsəgoosh
apricots	**alperces damascos** alPERSəsh daMASHkoosh
strawberries	**morangos** mooRANgoosh
raspberries	**framboesas** framboAYzash
water melon	**melancia** məlanSEEa

At the tobacconist

(For stamps, see 'Post Office' section.)

Have you got a postcard. . . .	**Tem um postal. . . .** tayng oong poshTAL
–of the palace?	**–do palácio?** –doo paLASyoo
–of the castle?	**–do castelo?** –doo kashTEloo
–of the cathedral?	**–da catedral?** –da kateDRAL

–of the hotel?	**–do hotel?**
	–doo oTEL
–of the park?	**–do parque?**
	–doo park
–of the sea?	**–do mar?**
	–doo mar
Have you got . . . ?	**Tem . . .?**
	tayng
Please give me a packet of. . . .	**Por favor, dê-me – um maço de (for cigarettes). . . .**
	fazh faVOOR DAY-mə oong MAsoo də
	–uma caixa de. . . .
	OOma KYSHa də
–un-tipped cigarettes.	**–cigarros sem filtro.**
	–seeGAhoosh sayng FEELtroo
–tipped cigarettes.	**–cigarros com filtro.**
	–seeGAhoosh kong FEELtroo
–cigarillos.	**–cigarrilhas.**
	–seegaHEELyash
–peppermints.	**–pastilhas de hortelã-pimenta.**
	–pashTEELyash də orteLÃ-peeMENta
–chewing-gum.	**–pastilhas elásticas.**
	–pashTEELyash LASHteekash
–tobacco (strong/mild/sweet).	**–tabaco (forte/fraco/aromático).**
	–taBAkoo (fort/FRAkoo/arooMAteekoo)
Please can I have. . . .	**Faz favor, dá-me. . . .**
	fazh faVOOR DA-mə
–some matches.	**–uma caixa de fósforos.**
	–OOma KYSHa də FOSHfooroosh
–some pipe-cleaners.	**–uns limpadores de cachimbo.**
	–oongsh leempaDOORəsh də kaSHEEMboo

–a bar of chocolate (milk/plain).	–uma tablete de chocolate (de leite/preto).
	–OOma tabLET də shokoLAT (də layt/PREtoo)
–a box of chocolates (big/small).	–uma caixa de bonbons/chocolates (grande/pequena).
	–OOma KYSHa də bongBONGSH/shokoLATəsh (grand/peKAYna)

Smoking

Have a cigarette./Do you smoke?	**Quer um cigarro?/Fuma?**
	kair oong seeGAhoo/FOOma
No, thanks, I don't smoke.	**Não obrigado, não fumo.**
	nowng obreeGAdoo nowng FOOmoo

At the chemist

The **'farmácia'** only stocks medical items. For perfume, make-up etc., you have to go to a **'perfumaria'** pərfoomaREEa.

Medical items

Please give me. . . .	**Faz favor dê-me. . . .**
	fazh faVOOR DAY-mə
–some cotton-wool.	–algodão.
	–algooDOWNG
–some disinfectant.	–desinfectante.
	–dəzeenfeTANT
–some antiseptic cream.	–creme antiséptico.
	–krem anteeSEPteekoo
–some sticking-plaster.	–adesivo.
	–adeZEEvoo
–a bandage.	–uma ligadura.
	–OOma leegaDOOra
–a crêpe bandage.	–uma ligadura de gaze.
	–OOma leegaDOOra də gazh

–some cough medicine.	**–um remédio para a tosse.**
	–oong reMAYDyoo PAra a toss
–some throat lozenges.	**–umas pastilhas para a garganta.**
	–OOmash pashTEELyash PAra a garGANTa
–some gargle.	**–um gargarejo.**
	–oong gargaREzhoo
–some anti-diarrhoea medicine.	**–um antiséptico intestinal.**
	–oong anteeSEPteekoo eenteshteeNAL
–some digestive pills.	**–umas pastilhas para a digestão.**
	–OOmash pashTEELyash PAra a deezheSHTOWNG
–some laxative.	**–um laxativo.**
	–oong laksaTEEvoo
–some insect repellant.	**–uma loção contra insectos.**
	–OOma looSOWNG KONTra eenSEToosh
–some sanitary towels.	**–toalhetes sanitários.**
	–twalYETəsh saneeTARyoosh
–some Tampax.	**–tampax.**
	–TAMpaks
–some paper tissues.	**–uns lenços de papel.**
	–oóngsh LENsoosh də paPEL
*What is wrong with you?	**De que é que se queixa?**
	də kee ay kə sə KAYsha

(See section on 'Medical Treatment' for describing symptoms.)

Can you prepare this prescription, please?	**Pode aviar-me esta receita faz favor?**
	pod avYAR-mə ESHtar SAYta fazh faVOOR

Cosmetic items

Please can I have. . . .	**Faz favor, dá-me. . . .** fazh faVOOR DA-mə
–some soap.	**–uns sabonetes.** –oongsh saboNETsh
–some toothpaste.	**–pasta de dentes.** –PASHta də DENTsh
–some shampoo.	**–champu.** –shamPOO
–some deodorant.	**–um desodorizante.** –oong dezodoreeZANT
–some make-up.	**–cosméticos.** –kozhMETeekoosh
–some suntan lotion.	**–um creme para bronzear.** –oong krem PAra bronzeAR
–some face cream.	**–um creme para a cara.** –oong krem PAra a KAra
–some lip cream.	**–um creme para os lábios.** –oong krem PAra oosh LAByoosh
–some hand cream.	**–um creme para as mãos.** –oong krem PAta ash mowsh
–some body lotion.	**–uma loção para o corpo.** –OOma looSOWNG PAra oo KOORpoo
–some razor blades.	**–umas lâminas para a barba.** –OOmash LAmeenash PAra a BARba
–some shaving cream.	**–um creme de barbear.** –oong krem də barbeAR
–some shaving soap.	**–um sabão de barbear.** –oong saBOWNG də barbeAR
–some after-shave.	**–um after-shave/–loção para a barba.** –oong 'after-shave'/loSOWNG PAra a BARba
–a razor.	**–uma navalha de barba.** –OOma naVALya də BARba **–uma gilette.** –OOma zheeLET

GENERAL NOTICES

Receitas	Prescriptions
Veneno	Poison
Só para uso externo	For External Use Only
Modo de emprego	Directions for Use

Clothes and accessories

*Can I help you?

Posso ajudá-lo?
POSsoo azhooDA-loo

No, I'm just looking, thank
you.

Não obrigado, estou só a ver.
nowng, obreeGAdoo shtoh soh a
vair

I'd like. . . .

Queria. . . .
kəREEa

–a coat (long).

–um casacão (comprido).
–oong kazaSOWNG
(komPREEdoo)

–a jacket (short).

–um casaco (curto).
–oong kaZAkoo (KOORtoo)

–a cardigan (medium-length).

**–casaco de malha (de meio
comprimento).**
–oong kaZAkoo də MALya (də
MAYoo kompreeMENToo)

–a dress (day).

–um vestido.
–oong veshTEEdoo

(evening).

(de noite).
oong veshTEEdoo (də noit)

(See Reference Section for colours)

*What size are you?

Qual é a sua medida?
kwal ay SOOa məDEEda

–(for shoes)?

Quanto calça?
KWANtoo KALsa

I'm size. . . .

Tamanho. . . .
taMANyoo

–(for shoes).	Calço. . . . KALsoo

(See following Conversion Tables for size equivalents.)

It's too. . . .	Está muito. . . . shta MWEENtoo
–tight.	–apertado. –apərTAdoo
–loose.	–largo. –LARgoo
–long.	–comprido. –komPREEdoo
–short.	–curto. –KOORtoo
–big.	–grande. –grand
It's too thick.	–É muito grosso. –ay MWEENtoo GROSsoo
It's too thin (light).	–É muito (leve). –ay MWEENtoo lev
It doesn't suit me.	Não me fica bem. nowng mə FEEka bayng
It doesn't fit me.	Não me serve. nowng mə sairv
Have you got it in. . . .	Tem em. . . . tayng ayng
–red?	–encarnado? –eenkarNAdoo
–brown?	–castanho? –kashTANyoo
–green?	–verde? –vaird
–blue?	–azul? –aZOOL
Do you keep . . . ?	Tem . . . ? tayng

Can you show me. . . .   **Pode mostrar-me. . . .**
     pod moshTRAR-mə

–skirts?   **–saias?**
     –SYash

–underwear?   **–roupa interior?**
     –ROHpa eentərYOR

–blouses?   **–blusas?**
     –BLOOzash

–nightwear?   **–roupa de dormir?**
     –ROHpa də doorMEER

This is just what I wanted.   **É mesmo isto o que queria.**
     ay MEZHmoo EESHtoo oo kə
         kəREEa

I'll take this.   **Eu levo isto.**
     Eoo LEVoo EESHtoo

How much is it?   **Quanto custa?**
     KWANtoo KOOSHta

Do you take credit cards?   **Aceitam cartões de crédito.**
     aSAYtang karTOengsh də
         KREdeetoo

Please may I have a receipt?   **Dá-me um recibo por favor?**
     DA-mə oong reSEEboo poor
         faVOOR

I'd like to change this.   **Gostaria de trocar isto.**
     goshtaREEa də troKAR
         EESHtoo

I bought it two days ago.   **Comprei isto há dois dias.**
     komPRAY EESHtoo a doish
         DEEash

–one week ago.   **–há uma semana.**
     –a OOma səMAna

Where can I buy . . .?   **Onde é que eu posso comprar . . .?**
     ONDee ay kee Eoo POSsoo
         komPRAR

Shoes

I'd like a pair of. . . .	**Queria um par de. . . .**
	kəREEa oong par də
–walking shoes.	**–sapatos de passeio.**
	–saPAtoosh də pasSAYoo
–smart shoes.	**–sapatos finos.**
	–saPAtoosh FEEnoosh
–beach shoes.	**–sapatos de praia.**
	–saPAtoosh də PRYa
–beach sandals.	**–sandálias de praia.**
	–sanDALyash də PRYa
–sandals.	**–sandálias.**
	–sanDALyash
–tennis shoes.	**–sapatos de ténis.**
	–saPAtoosh də TENees
–boots.	**–botas.**
	–BOtash
I'm afraid I don't like. . . .	**Não gosto muito. . . .**
	nowng GOSHtoo MWEENtoo
–the style.	**–do estilo.**
	–doo SHTEEloo
–the colour.	**–da côr.**
	–da kohr
The heels are too high.	**Os saltos são muito altos.**
	oosh SALtoosh sowng MWEENtoo ALtoosh
–too low.	**–muito baixos.**
	–MWEENtoo BYshoosh
They're too small.	**Estão apertados.**
	shtowng apərTAdoosh
–too big.	**–grandes.**
	–GRANDəsh

VOCABULARY

socks	peúgas/meias	peOOgash/MAYash
underpants (*ladies'*)	cuecas	KWEkash
(*men's*)	cuecas	KWEkash

stockings	**meias** MAYash
tights	**meia-calça** MAYa-KALsa
bra	**soutien** sootYANG
petticoat	**petticoat/combinação** petticoat/ kombeenaSOWNG
vest	**camisola** kameeZOla
shirt	**camisa** kaMEEza
blouse	**blusa** BLOOza
cardigan	**casaco de malha** kaZAkoo də MALya
pullover	**pullover** pullover
jacket	**casaco** kaZAkoo
skirt	**saia** SYa
trousers (*ladies'*)	**calças** KALsash
(*men's*)	**calças** KALsash
trouser suit	**fato** FAtoo
suit (*ladies'*)	**vestido** veshTEEdoo
(*men's*)	**fato** FAtoo
nightdress	**camisa de noite** kaMEEza do noit
pyjamas	**pijama** peeZHAma
tie	**gravata** graVAta
dress	**vestido** veshTEEdoo
long dress	**vestido comprido** veshTEEdoo comPREEdoo
scarf	**lenço** LENsoo
hat	**chapéu** shaPAYoo
cap	**boné** boNAY
raincoat	**gabardine** gabarDEEN
coat	**casaco comprido** KaZAkoo koomPREEdoo
umbrella	**chapéu de chuva** shaPAYoo
bikini	**bikini** beeKEEnee
swimming costume	**fato de banho** FAtoo də BANyoo
swimming trunks	**calções de banho** kalSOengsh də BANyoo
tee-shirt	**tee-shirt** tee-shirt
shorts	**calções** kalSOengsh

Some common materials

What's it made of?	De que é que é feito? də kee ay kee ay FAYtoo
I'd like it in. . . .	Eu queria em. . . . Eoo kəREEa ayng
wool	lã la
cotton	algodão algooDOWNG
nylon	nylon nyLON
acrylic	acrílico aKREEleekoo
fur	peles PELsh
leather	cabedal kabəDAL
suede	camurça kaMOORsa
silk	seda SEda
corduroy	bombazina/belbutina bombaZEEna/ bəlbooTEEna
velvet	veludo veLOOdoo
linen	linho LEENyoo

Photography

I'd like . . . please.	Queria . . . por favor. kəREEa poor faVOOR
–a film for this camera	–um rolo para esta máquina –oong ROloo PAra ESHta MAkeena
–a black and white film	–um rolo a preto a branco –oong ROloo a PRAYtoo ee BRANkoo
–a colour print film	–um rolo de côres –oong ROloo də KOHRəsh
–a colour slide film	–um rolo de diapositivos a côres –oong ROloo də deeapozeeTEEvoosh a KOHRəsh

–an 8-mm film

–um filme de oito milímetros
–oong feelm də OIToo meeLEEmetroosh

–a 35-mm film

–um filme de trinta e cinco milímetros
–oong feelm de trinta e cinco meeLEEmetroosh

–some flash bulbs

–uns flashes
–oongsh FLASHəsh

with twenty exposures.

de vinte fotografias.
də veent fotograFEEash

with thirty-six exposures.

de trinta e seis fotografias.
də TREENTa ee saysh fotograFEEash

Do you print photos?

Imprimem/revelam fotografias aqui?
eemPREEmayng/rəVELang fotograFEEash aKEE

How much does it cost?

Quanto custa?
KWANtoo KOOSHta

Is developing included?

A revelação está incluída?
a revəlaSOWNG shta eenklooEEda

I'd like this film developed.

Queria deixar este filme a revelar.
kəREEa daySHAR esht feelm a revəLAR

–only into negatives.

–só negativos.
–soh negaTEEvoosh

I'd like this photo enlarged.

Queria ampliar esta fotografia.
kəREEa amplYAR ESHta fotograFEEa

With a glossy/matt finish.

Com superficie brilhante/mate.
kong soopərFEEsyə breelYANT/ mat

I'd like (four) prints of this one.

Queria (quatro) fotografias desta.
kəREEa (KWATroo) fotograFEEash DESHta

When will it be ready?	**Quando é que está pronta?**
	KWANdoo ay kee shta PRONta
When will they be ready?	**Quando é que estão prontas?**
	KWANdoo ay kee SHTOWNG
	PRONtash
Please can you mend my camera?	**Posso deixar esta máquina a arranjar?**
	POSsoo daySHAR ESHta MAkeena a ahanZHAR
Please can you take out the film?	**Pode tirar o filme para fora?**
	pod teeRAR oo feelm PAra FOra
The film is stuck.	**O filme está encravado.**
	oo feelm shta eenkraVAdoo

Books and stationery

Do you keep English newspapers?	**Tem algum jornal Inglês?**
	tayng alGOONG zhorNAL eenGLAYSH
Do you have any English books?	**Tem algum livro inglês?**
	tayng alGOONG LEEvroo eenGLAYSH
Do you sell road maps?	**Tem algum mapa das estradas?**
	tayng alGOONG MApa dash əSHTRAdash
I'd like....	**Queria....**
	kəREEa
–a map.	–**um mapa.**
	–oong MApa
–a guide-book.	–**um guia.**
	–oong GEEa
–a post-card.	–**um postal.**
	–oong poshTAL
–a notebook.	–**um bloco de notas.**
	–oong BLOkoo də NOtash

–an exercise book.

–um caderno de exercícios.
–oong kaDAIRnoo
  de zərSEESyoosh

–a pen.

–uma caneta.
–OOma kaNETa

–a biro.

–uma esferográfica.
–OOma shferooGRAfeeka

–a pencil.

–um lápis.
–oong LApeesh

–a rubber.

–uma borracha.
–OOma bəHAsha

–some writing-paper.

–papel de carta.
–paPEL də KARta

–some ink.

–tinta de caneta.
–TEENta də kaNETa

–some envelopes.

–uns envelopes.
–oongsh eenvəLOPəsh

–some sellotape.

–fita-cola.
–FEEta-KOla

–some string.

–um cordel.
–oong korDEL

–some brown paper.

–papel pardo.
–paPEL PARdoo

–some tie-on labels.

–umas etiquetas de atar.
–OOmash eteeKETash də aTAR

–some stick-on labels.

–umas etiquetas autocolantes.
–OOmash eteeKETash
  / owtookooLANTSH

Food and Wine

The Portuguese are justifiably proud of their food and wine.

Food
Particularly good are the fresh fish and shell-fish dishes: the variety and availability of fish and the various ways of serving them make for a wide choice on the menu. Always ask first for the local speciality.

Pork is the most usual meat and is served in many different and delicious ways.

Note: 'bife' means a steak, but not necessarily a beef steak: it could be veal or even fish.

Rice is the staple vegetable, but there are always others in season.

Cheese is usually made from ewe's milk ('Queijo da Serra', best between October and May) or goat's milk ('cabreiro'). Different regions have their own speciality.

There is a wide variety of pastries; again each locality has its speciality.

Wine
Portugal produces very good red, rosé or white wines. Usually a carafe of house wine is included in a fixed price meal; this will be a local wine probably, and it is interesting to compare the wines of the different regions.

The 'vinhos verdes' (literally green wines, because the grapes are green even when ripe) are not very alcoholic, but sparkling and refreshing. They vary from white to red.

Madeira wine, produced in the island of the same name which belongs to Portugal, is a sweet wine but it has different degrees of sweetness. Some are drunk as aperitif wines and some as dessert wines. Dishes cooked in sauces made with Madeira wine are delicious.

Last but by no means least, port. Portugal is of course the country of origin of port wine, so you must try some during your stay. You can have white port, which is dry, as an aperitif, or the sweet or medium sweet red as a liqueur at the end of the meal.

For characteristics of Brazilian food see the end of the Menu section.

Menu

Here is a list of some of the dishes you will probably find on a Portuguese menu. Never be afraid to ask the waiter to explain what a dish consists of. It's much better to know what you're going to get than to be perhaps disappointed.

Hors d'oeuvres	*Hors d'oeuvres*
Acepipes variados	Plate of various hors d'oeuvres
Empadinhas	Little home-made pies
Empadinhas de atum	Tuna-fish pies
Empadinhas de camarão	Shrimp/prawn pies
Empadinhas de galinha	Chicken pies
Cocktail de camarão	Prawn cocktail
Presunto	Smoked raw ham
Presunto com figos	Smoked raw ham with figs
Arroz de tomate	Rice with tomato and onions

Sopas	*Soups*
Sopa de peixe	Fish soup
Sopa de mariscos	Seafood soup (shellfish)
Sopa de grão	Chick-pea soup
Sopa de feijão	Red bean and cabbage soup
Canja de galinha	Clear chicken soup with rice
Caldo verde	Potato and green cabbage soup with slices of black pudding (tora) or spicy sausage (chouriço)

Sopas	*Soups*
Açorda	Bread soup
Açorda de alho	Bread soup with garlic and herbs
Gaspacho	A cold soup, made of tomato, onion, pimento, cucumber and herbs

Carne	*Meat*
Porco assado	Roast pork
Leitão assado	Roast sucking pig
Carne de porco à alentejana	Pork marinated in wine, cooked in tomato and onions and garnished with oysters
Cozido à Portuguesa	Stew of beef, ham, sausage, vegetables, potatoes and rice
Dobrada	Pork or beef tripe cooked with haricot beans
Bife	Steak
Costeletas (de borrego)	Lamb cutlets
Carne de vaca assada	Roast beef
Frango assado	Roast chicken
Arroz de frango	Fried chicken cooked in white wine with ham and rice
Coelho assado	Rabbit roast with onions and white wine
Alheiras	Chicken with spiced sausage
Arroz de pato	Duck with rice
Iscas	Liver

Legumes	*Vegetables*
Batatas	Potatoes
Cenouras	Carrots
Cogumelos	Mushrooms
Favas	Broad beans
Ervilhas	Peas
Couve	Cabbage
Legumes mistos	Mixed vegetables

Legumes	*Vegetables*
Salada mista	Mixed salad
Salada	Green salad

Doces/Sobremesa	*Desserts*
Pudim flan	Similar to cream caramel
Arroz doce	Rice pudding
Gelado	Ice cream
Bolo	Cake/Pastry
Fruta fresca	Fresh fruit
Café	Coffee

Ovos	*Eggs*
Ovos cozidos	Boiled eggs
Ovos à Minhota	Baked eggs with tomato and onions
Omelete	Omelette
Omelete de camarões	Shrimp omelette
Omelete de chourico	Smoked sausage omelette
Omelete de presunto	Smoked ham omelette

Peixe e Marisco	*Fish and seafood*
Bacalhau	Dried salted cod
Bacalhau cozido	Boiled cod with potatoes and vegetables
Bacalhau à Brás	Dried cod fried with potatoes and onions then cooked in beaten egg
Bacalhau à Gomes de Sá	Cod with olives, garlic, onions, parsley and hard-boiled eggs
Caldeirada	Fish stew
Atum	Tuna fish (fresh)
Sardinhas	Sardines
Salmão	Salmon
Lulas	Squid
Lulas recheadas	Squid, stuffed and cooked in tomato sauce
Pescada	Hake
Lagosta	Crayfish

Peixe e Marisco	Fish and seafood
Ostras	Oysters
Mexilhões	Mussels
Ameijoas	Clams

Brazilian food and drink

Brazilian food differs from Portuguese in that there is wider variety of home-grown products, *e.g.* beans (black, brown or red), nuts, coconuts, mangoes, pineapples, pawpaws etc. It is also generally spicier: ginger and chilis are common ingredients. The distinctive flavour of some dishes comes from the coconut milk or yellow palm oil in which the food is cooked.

Churrascarias are restaurants which specialise in barbecued food.

Here are a few Brazilian dishes you would find on a menu there, just to whet your appetite:

Feijoada	This is the most popular dish in Brazil, traditionally eaten on Wednesdays and Saturdays. A 'pot-pourri' of meats and sausages, cooked with black beans, served with rice and fresh oranges
Vatapá	A speciality from the North-East of Brazil: fish and prawns cooked in coconut milk, dendê (yellow palm) oil, ginger, peanuts and other seasonings
Churrasco mixto	Mixed barbecue (mainly beef, pork and sausages)
Bacalhau com leite de côco	Cod stewed in coconut milk
Cocada	A dessert made from grated coconut
Goiabada	A thick jelly made of guavas
Sorvete	Ice-cream; this is often made from tropical fruits

Coffee

Of course, Brazil produces its own coffee. It is generally very strong like 'espresso' coffee and is served black with sugar to take the bitter taste away.

Drinks

Brazilians drink more beer than the Portuguese as their climate requires somewhat more thirst-quenching drinks. They also have some very exotic tropical drinks which are very refreshing. Some good wines are produced in some of the regions of Brazil.

Restaurants, Cafés and Bars

Lunch (o almoço) is served from 1.00 to 3.00 p.m. in both Portugal and Brazil. Dinner in an ordinary restaurant is served from about 7.30 to 9.00 p.m. but in a **Casa de Fado** (see Entertainment section) it is served later, about 9.30, with the Fado starting at about 10.30. Brazilians eat dinner much later: any time between 8.00 and 11.00 p.m.

Apart from the ordinary restaurants you can find excellent regional specialities in the **Pousadas** (state-owned hotels) or **Estalagens** (privately owned hotels). The **Casas de Fado** also serve Portuguese specialities (see the Menu section).

You can always get a cup of coffee or tea and a cake in a **Confeitaria** or **Pasteleria** (a cake-shop), or if you need something stronger a **Café-Bar** will provide alcoholic drinks, as well as coffee, snacks etc.

Reserving a table

Can you recommend a good restaurant?

Pode recomendar-me um bom restaurante?

pod rekomenDAR-mə oong bong rəshtowRANT

I'd like to book a table.	**Queria reservar uma mesa.**
	kəREEa rezərVAR OOma **MEza**
For four people.	**Para quatro pessoas.**
	PAra KWATroo pesSOash
At 8.00 o'clock.	**Para as oito horas.**
	PAra ash OItoo Orash
*I'm sorry, we're all booked up tonight.	**Tenho muita pena mas já não temos mesas para esta noite.**
	TENyoo MWEENta PAYna mash zha nowng TAYmoosh MEzash PAra ESHta noit
I've reserved a table.	**Tenho uma mesa reservada.**
	TENyoo OOma MEza rezərVAda
My name is. . . .	**O meu nome é. . . .**
	oo MEoo nom ay
Have you a table for two?	**Tem uma mesa para duas pessoas?**
	tayng OOma MEza PAra DOOash pesSOash
We're in a hurry.	**Estamos cheios de pressa.**
	SHTAmoosh SHAYoosh də PRESsa

Ordering your meal
(See the previous section for an example of a typical menu.)

Can we see the menu, please?	**Dá-nos a ementa por favor?**
	DA-noosh a eeMENta poor faVOOR
Can I have the wine-list?	**Dá-me a carta dos vinhos?**
	DA-mə a KARta doosh VEENyoosh
What's this?	**O que é isto?**
	oo kee ay EESHtoo
What do you recommend?	**O que é que nos recomenda?**
	oo kee ay kə noosh rekooMENda

Are vegetables included?	**Os legumes estão incluídos?** oosh leGOOMəsh shtowng eenklooEEdoosh
Is the drink included?	**As bebidas estão incluídas?** ash bəBEEdash shtowng eenklooEEdoosh
I'll have. . . .	**Eu quero. . . .** Eoo KAIRoo
*How do you like your steak done?	**Como é que quer o seu bife?** KOMoo ay kə kair oo SEoo beef
Rare.	**Mal passado.** mal pasSAdoo
Medium rare.	**Normal.** noorMAL
Well done.	**Bem passado.** bayng pasSAdoo
Do you sell wine by the glass?	**Servem vinho a copo?** sərVAYNG VEENyoo a KOpoo
We'd like. . . .	**Queremos. . . .** kəRAYmoosh
–a bottle of local wine.	**–uma garrafa de vinho da região.** –OOma gaHAfa də VEENyoo da rəzhYOWNG
–a carafe of local wine.	**–um jarro de vinho da região.** –oong ZHAhoo də VEENyoo da rəzhYOWNG
–some red wine.	**–vinho tinto.** –VEENyoo TEENtoo
–some white wine.	**–vinho branco.** –VEENyoo BRANkoo
–some rosé.	**–rosé.** –roZAY
–a glass of beer.	**–uma cerveja.** –OOma sərVAYzha
–some water.	**–água.** –AGwa

Could I have some more . . .?	**Pode trazer mais . . .?** pod traZAIR mysh

Complaints and questions

This isn't what I ordered.	**Isto não é o que eu pedi.** EESHtoo nowng ay oo kee Eoo peDEE
There's a mistake.	**Há um engano.** a oong eenGAnoo
This is dirty.	**Isto está sujo.** EESHtoo shta SOOzhoo
–cold.	**–frio.** –FREEoo
–stale.	**–estragado.** –shtraGAdoo
Please change the. . . .	**Faz favor mude a. . . .** fazh faVOOR mood a
The fish is bad.	**O peixe não está bom.** oo paysh nowng shta bong
–not cooked.	**–está cru.** –shta kroo
I'd like to see the manager.	**Queria falar com o gerente.** kəREEa faLAR kong oo zheRENT
*We've run out of. . . .	**Já não temos. . . .** zha nowng TAYmoosh
Where's the lavatory?	**Onde é a casa de banho?** ONDee ay a KAza də BANyoo

Paying the bill

Can I have the bill, please?	**Faz favor, traz-me a conta?** fazh faVOOR TRAZH-mə a KONta
What is this charge for?	**O que é este preço?** oo kee ay ESHTə PREsoo

I think there's a mistake.	**Parece-me que há um engano.** paRES-mə kee a oong eenGAnoo
I didn't have. . . .	**Eu não comi. . . .** Eoo nowng koMEE
I didn't order. . . .	**Eu não pedi. . . .** Eoo nowng peDEE
Is service included?	**O serviço está incluído?** oo sərVEEsoo shta eenklooEEdoo
Thank you very much.	**Muito obrigado.** MEEENtoo obreeGAdoo
It was a very good meal.	**Estava tudo óptimo.** SHTAva TOOdoo OPteemoo
Goodbye.	**Adeus.** aDEoosh

VOCABULARY

ashtray	**cinzeiro** seenZAIRoo
glass	**copo** KOpoo
knife	**faca** FAka
fork	**garfo** GARfoo
spoon	**colher** kolYAIR
teaspoon	**colher de chá** kolYAIR də sha
cup	**chávena** SHAvena
plate	**prato** PRAtoo
napkin	**guardanapo** gwardaNApoo
salt	**sal** sal
pepper	**pimenta** peeMENta
mustard	**mostarda** moshTARda
salad dressing	**molho de salada** MOLyoo də saLAda
sauce	**molho** MOLyoo
tea	**chá** sha
coffee	**café** kaFAY
mineral water	**água mineral** AGwa meenəRAL
milk	**leite** layt
brandy	**brandy** BRANdee

sherry	**xerez** SHErəzh
lemonade	**limonada** leemoNAda
orange squash	**laranjada** laranZHAda
fruit juice	**sumo de fruta** SOOmoo də FROOta
fizzy	**gasosa** gaZOza
still	**sem gas** sayng gash
raw	**cru** kroo

(See the section 'In a food shop' for the names of meats, fruit, etc.)

Methods of cooking

These words will appear on the menu as descriptions of the way the meat or fish has been cooked:

fumado	smoked
fooMAdoo	
cozido no forno	baked
koZEEdoo noo FOORnoo	
frito	fried
FREEtoo	
guisado	braised
geeZAdoo	
cozido	boiled
koZEEdoo	
recheado	stuffed
reshayAdoo	
assado	roast
asSAdoo	
grelhado	grilled
grəlYAdoo	

At the Hairdresser or Barber

I'd like to make an appointment for. . . .

Queria fazer uma marcação para. . . .

kəREEa faZAIR OOma markaSOWNG PAra

I'd like my hair. . . .

Queria que me. . . .

kəREEa kə mə

–cut.

–cortasse o cabelo.

–korTASS oo kaBEloo

–washed.

–lavasse a cabelo.

–laVASS oo kaBEloo

–trimmed.

–aparasse as pontas.

–apaRASS ash PONtash

–set.

–arranjasse o cabelo.

–ahanZHASS oo kaBEloo

–re-styled.

–fizesse um novo penteado.

–feeZESS oong NOvoo penteAdoo

–permed.

–fizesse uma permanente.

–feeZESS OOma permaNENT

–straightened.

–alizasse o cabelo.

–aleeZASS oo kaBEloo

–tinted.

–pintasse o cabelo.

–peenTASS oo kaBEloo

–dyed.

–pintasse o cabelo (de outra côr).

–peenTASS oo kaBEloo (də OHtra kohr)

–blow-dried.

–secasse o cabelo à mão.

–seKASS oo kaBEloo a mowng

*How much do you want cut?

De que tamanho é que quer o cabelo?

də kə taMANyoo ay kə kair oo kaBEloo

Not much.	**Corte pouco.**
	kort POHkoo
A lot.	**Corte muito.**
	kort MWEENtoo
Not too short.	**Não muito curto.**
	nowng MWEENtoo KOORtoo
Not very short on top.	**Não muito curto em cima.**
	nowng MWEENtoo KOORtoo ayng SEEma
–at the sides.	**dos lados.**
	doosh LAdoosh
That's enough.	**Já chega.**
	zha SHEga
Please cut more off the back.	**Corte mais atrás, por favor.**
	kort mysh aTRASH, poor faVOOR
–the sides.	**–dos lados.**
	–doosh LAdoosh
–the top.	**–em cima.**
	–ayng SEEma
I'm in a hurry.	**Tenho muita pressa.**
	TENyoo MWEENta PRESSsa
The drier is too hot.	**O secador está muito quente.**
	oo sekaDOOR shta MWEENtoo kent
–too cold.	**–muito frio.**
	–MWEENtoo FREEoo
I'd like. . . .	**Queria. . . .**
	kəREEa
–a shave.	**–fazer a barba.**
	–faZAIR a BARba
–a manicure.	**–arranjar as unhas.**
	–ahanZHAR ash OONyash
–some nail-polish.	**–verniz.**
	–vərNEESH

–some setting-lotion.

–some conditioner.

–uma loção para o cabelo.
–OOma looSOWNG PAra oo
kaBEloo

–um condicionador para o cabelo.
–oong kondeesyonaDOOR PAra
oo kaBEloo

Laundry/Dry-cleaning

Please can you clean . . . ?	**Queria deixar . . . a limpar?** kəREEa daySHAR . . . a leemPAR
–these clothes.	**–esta roupa** –ESHta ROHpa
–this coat.	**–este casacão** –esht kazaKOWNG
–this raincoat.	**–esta gabardine** –ESHta gaberDEEN
–this skirt.	**–esta saia** –ESHta SYa
–this jacket.	**–este casaco** –esht kaZAkoo
–these trousers.	**–estas calças** –ESHtash KALsash
I'd like . . . washed.	**Queria deixar . . . a lavar.** kəREEa daySHAR a laVAR
Please can you remove this stain?	**Consegue tirar esta nódoa?** konSEG teeRAR ESHta NOHdooa
Please re-proof. . . .	**Pode impermeabilizar. . . .** pod eempərmeabeeleeZAR
–mend	**–coser. . . .** –koZAIR
–press	**–engomar** –engooMAR
Can you launder these shirts, please?	**Pode lavar estas camisas, por favor?** pod laVAR ESHtash kaMEEzash poor faVOOR

I need it as soon as possible.	**Preciso disso o mais depressa possível.**
	preSEEzoo DEESsoo oo mysh dəPRESsa posSEEvel
Can you do it express?	**Pode fazê-lo em expresso?**
	pod faZAY-loo ayng esPRESsoo
When will it be ready?	**Quando é que está pronto?**
	KWANdoo ay kee shta PRONtoo
When will they be ready?	**Quando é que estão prontas?**
	KWANdoo ay que shtowng PRONtash
This is still dirty.	**Isto ainda está sujo.**
	EESHtoo aEENda shta SOOzhoo
I don't want to pay.	**Não quero pagar.**
	nowng KAIRoo paGAR

At the Bank

Bank opening hours are 9.30 a.m. to 12.00 and 2.00 to 4.00 p.m. On Saturdays they are only open until 11.30 a.m.

Exchange offices (**'cambios'**) are open from 9.30 a.m. to 6.00 p.m. On Saturdays they close at 1.00 p.m.

Remember always to take your passport with you.

It's advisable to cash enough money at a bank or cambio as most hotels and shops do not like foreign currency and have not got the facilities for exchange.

Please change this into. . . .	**Troque-me isto em . . . por favor.** TROK-mə EESHtoo ayng . . . poor faVOOR
Please cash these cheques.	**Queria levantar estes cheques.** kəREEa ləvanTAR ESHtəsh SHEKəsh
Can I have it in notes, please?	**Queria em notas por favor.** kəREEa ayng NOtash por faVOOR
Can I have it in small change, please?	**Queria em troco pequeno poor favor.** kəREEa ayng TROKoo peKAYnoo poor faVOOR
Has my bank transfer arrived?	**Já chegou a transferencia do meu banco?** zha sheGOH a transfeRENSya doo MEoo BANkoo
Can you cable my bank?	**Pode telegrafar ao meu banco?** pod teləgraFAR Aoo MEoo BANkoo
How long will it take?	**Quanto tempo demora?** KWANtoo TEMpoo dəMORa

*Up to a week.   Cerca de uma semana.
                                 SAIRka DOOMa səMAna

(See 'Reference Section' for numbers and dates.)

At the Post Office

Post Offices are called CTT (**Correios, Telégrafos e Telefones**). They are usually open from 8.00 a.m. to noon and from 3.00 to 7.00 p.m.

Letter-boxes are painted red. (In Brazil there are no letter-boxes: you have to post your letter in the Post Office.)

Stamps (**selos**) have to be bought at the Post Office; the larger hotels sometimes sell them at the reception desk.

How much is a letter for England?	**Quanto é uma carta para Inglaterra?** KWANtoo ay OOma KARta PAra eenglaTEha
How much is a postcard to England?	**Quanto é um postal para Inglaterra?** KWANtoo ay oong poshTAL PAra eenglaTEha

(See 'Reference Section' for other countries.)

Please give me	**Queria** kəREEa
–a . . . stamp.	**– umsêlo de. . . .** –oong SAYloo də
–an aerogramme.	**–um aerograma.** –oong a-AIRooGRAma
–a telegram form.	**–um impresso de telegramas.** –oong eemPRESsoo də teləGRAmash
I want to send . . . to. . . .	**Queria mandar . . . para. . . .** kəREEa manDAR . . . PAra
–a telegram.	**–um telegrama.** –oong teləGRAma
–a parcel.	**–uma encomenda.** –OOma eenkoMENda

–an international money order.
–um vale de correio internacional.
–oong val də koHAYoo
   eentərnasyoNAL

How much is it per word?
Quanto é por palavra?
KWANtoo ay poor paLAvra

Reply paid.
Resposta paga.
rəshPOSHta PAga

Can I have a customs
   declaration form?
**Dá-me um impresso de
   declaração de alfândega?**
DA-mə oong eemPRESsoo də
   dəklaraSOWNG də
   alFANdəga

I'd like to send this. . . .
Queria mandar isto. . . .
kəREEa manDAR EESHtoo

–surface mail.
–por terra.
–poor TEha

–air mail.
–por avião.
–poor avYOWNG

–registered.
–registado.
rəzheeSHTAdoo

–express.
–expresso.
eeshPRESsoo

–recorded delivery.
–com aviso de recepção.
–kong aVEEzoo də rəseSOWNG

WRITTEN POSTAL INSTRUCTIONS

Não dobrar   Do not bend
nowng doBRAR
Frágil   Fragile
FRAzheel
Urgente   Urgent
oorZHENT

Poste Restante

Don't forget to take your passport with you when you go to collect any mail.

Letters to be kept for you by the local central post office should be addressed **Posta Restante** before the name of the locality.

Where's the Poste Restante counter?	**Onde é o balcão da Posta Restante?** ONDee ay oo balKOWNG da POSHta reshTANT
Is there any post for me?	**Há algum correio para mim?** a alGOONG koHAYoo PAra meeng
*What's your name?	**Como se chama?** KOmoo sə SHAma
My name is. . . .	**Chamo-me. . . .** SHAmoo-mə
*Show me your passport?	**Mostra-me o seu passaporte.** MOSHtra-mə oo SEoo passaPORT
When's the next delivery?	**Quando chega o próximo correio?** KWANdoo SHEGa oo PROSseemoo koHAYoo
When's the last delivery today?	**A que horas é a última distribuição de correio?** a kee Orash ay a OOLteema deeshtreebweeSOWNG də koHAYoo
Could you please forward my mail?	**Pode enviar-me a minha correspondência?** pod eenvYAR-mə a MEENya koheshponDAYNSya

Here's my forwarding address.

Aqui tem a morada para o envio da minha correspondência.
aKEE tayng a moRAda PAra oo eenVEEdoo da MEENya koheshponDAYNSya

---

Public phone-boxes in Portugal are painted red.

Local dialling codes are listed in the telephone directory (**lista telefónica**).

When you give a telephone number to the operator, say each number as a unit, *e.g.* 328 . . . **três, dois, oito.** . . .

When doing this, Brazilians say **meia** instead of **seis** for six.

Is there a telephone here?	**Há aqui algum telefone?** a aKEE alGOONG teləFON
Please may I use the 'phone?	**Posso fazer um telefonema por favor?** POSsoo faZAIR oong teləfoNEma poor faVOOR
Where's the nearest telephone-box?	**Onde é a cabina de telefone mais próxima?** ONDee ay a kaBEEna də teləFON mysh PROSseema

Direct dialling

Hello, this is. . . .	**Está lá, aqui fala.** . . . shta la, aKEE FAla
Can I speak to . . . please?	**Posso falar com . . . por favor?** POSsoo faLAR kong poor faVOOR
Hold on, please.	**Espere um momento, por favor.** shpair oong mooMENtoo poor faVOOR
Extension . . . please.	**Extensão . . . por favor.** eeshtenSOWNG poor faVOOR

Can I leave a message, please?	**Posso deixar um recado por favor?**
	POSsoo daySHAR oong reKAdoo poor faVOOR
Sorry, I've got the wrong number.	**Desculpe, enganei-me no número.**
	dəshKOOP, eengaNAY-mə noo NOOməroo
*I'll call you back.	**Eu devolvo-lhe a chamada.**
	Eoo dəVOLvoo-lyə a shaMAda
*There's no reply.	**Não atende.**
	nowng aTEND
I'll try again later.	**Eu volto a tentar mais tarde.**
	Eoo VOLtoo a tenTAR mysh tard
*Who's speaking?	**Quem fala?**
	kayng FAla
Goodbye.	**Adeus.**
	aDEoosh

Calls made via the operator

I'd like to make a personal call to. . . .	**Queria uma chamada pessoal para. . . .**
	kəREEa OOma shaMAda pessoAL PAra
I'd like to make a reverse charge call to. . . .	**Queria uma chamada para . . . a pagar pelo destinatário.**
	kəREEa OOma shaMAda PAra . . . a paGAR PEloo deshteenaTARyoo
*What's your number?	**Qual é o número do seu telefone?**
	kwal ay oo NOOməroo doo SEoo teləFON

I'd like to make a call to England.	**Queria uma chamada para Inglaterra.**
	kəREEa OOma shaMAda PAra eenglaTEha
Can I book a call for . . . o'clock?	**Posso marcar uma chamada para as . . . horas?**
	POSsoo marKAR OOma shaMAda PAra ash . . . Orash
What's the delay? (i.e. how long)	**Quanto tempo demora?**
	KWANtoo TEMpoo dəMOra
How much will it cost?	**Quanto é que custa?**
	KWANtoo ay kə KOOSHta
For . . . minutes.	**Por . . . minutos.**
	poor meeNOOtoosh
*The line's engaged.	**O número que deseja estáa falar.**
	oo NOOməroo kə dəZEZHa shta a faLAR
*Replace the receiver.	**Desligue o telefone.**
	dəzLEEG oo teləFON
*Don't replace the receiver.	**Não desligue.**
	nowng dəzLEEG
I've been cut off.	**Cortaram-me a chamada.**
	koorTARang-mə a shaMAda
Please could you reconnect me?	**Pode-me tornar a ligar.**
	pod-mə toorNAR a leeGAR
The 'phone's out of order.	**O telefone está avariado.**
	oo teləFON shta avarYAdoo

Medical Treatment

It is advisable to take out a comprehensive medical insurance policy before you go to Portugal. There is no national health service there and it is not a member of the EEC. Any travel agent can arrange this for you.

At the doctor's

Where's the nearest doctor?	**Onde é o consultório médico mais próximo?** ONDee ay oo konsoolTORyoo MEdeekoo mysh PROSseemoo
Must I make an appointment?	**Tenho que marcar consulta?** TENyoo ke marKAR konSOOLta
Does he speak English?	**Ele fala inglês?** Elə FAla eenGLAYSH
It's an emergency.	**É uma emergência.** áy OOma eemərZHAYNSya
Ring for an ambulance.	**Chame uma ambulância.** sham OOma ambooLANSya

Most frequent complaints

My . . . aches.	**Dói-me. . . .** DOI-mə
–stomach	–o estômago. –oo SHTOmagoo
–chest	–o peito. –oo PAYtoo
–ear	–o ouvido. –oo ohVEEdoo
–head	–a cabeça. –a kaBEsa

–back	**–as costas.**
	–ash KOOSHtash
I've got a temperature.	**Tenho febre.**
	TENyoo FEBrə
I've got a. . . .	**Tenho. . . .**
	TENyoo
–cough.	**–tosse.**
	–toss
–sore throat.	**–a garganta inflamada.**
	–a garGANta eenflaMAda
I've got a cold.	**Estou constipado.**
	shtoh konshteePAdoo
–migraine.	**–uma enxaqueca.**
	–OOmaa eenshaKEka
–stiff neck.	**–um torcicolo.**
	–oong toorseeKOloo
–rash.	**–uma erupção na pele.**
	–OOma eroopSOWNG na pel
I've got. . . .	**Estou com. . . .**
	shtoh kong
–constipation.	**–prisão de ventre.**
	–preSOWNG də VENTrə
–indigestion.	**–uma indigestão.**
	–OOma eendeezheSHTOWNG
–cramp.	**–uma cãibra.**
	–OOma KYbra
–sunstroke.	**–uma insolação.**
	–OOma eensolaSOWNG
I feel. . . .	**Sinto-me. . . .**
	SEENtoo-mə
–dizzy.	**–com tonturas.**
	–kong tonTOOrash
–faint.	**–a desmaiar.**
	–a dəshmyYAR
–sick.	**–mal.**
	–mal

I can't. . . .	**Não consigo. . . .**
	nowng konSEEgoo
–sleep.	**–dormir.**
	–doorMEER
–breathe.	**–respirar.**
	–reshpeeRAR
–eat anything.	**–comer nada.**
	–kooMAIR NAda
–pass water.	**–verter água.**
	–vairTAIR AGwa
I think I've got. . . .	**Tenho a impressão que. . . .**
	TENyoo a eempresSOWNG kee
–food poisoning.	**–apanhei uma intoxicação alimentar.**
	apanYAY OOma eentosseekaSOWNG aleemenTAR
–urinary infection.	**–tenho uma infecção urinária.**
	TENyoo OOma eenfeSOWNG ooreeNARya
–sinusitis.	**–tenho sinusíte.**
	TENyoo seenooSEET
I've twisted my. . . .	**Torci. . . .**
	toorSEE
–wrist.	**–o pulso.**
	–oo POOLsoo
–arm.	**–o braço.**
	–oo BRAsoo
–leg.	**–a perna.**
	–a PAIRna
–ankle.	**–o tornozelo.**
	–o toornooZEloo
I've twisted my back.	**–Dei um jeito nas costas.**
	–day oong ZHAYtoo nash KOSHtash
*Where does it hurt?	**Onde é que dói?**
	ONDee ay kə doi

*Tell me when it hurts.	**Diga-me quando doer.** DEEga-mə KWANdoo dwair
*How long has it been like this?	**Há quanto tempo está assim?** a KWANtoo TEMpoo shta aSEENG

Personal details and requests

Can I have a prescription for . . .?	**Pode passar-me uma receita para . . .?** pod pasSAR-mə OOma reSAYta PAra
Can you inoculate me against . . .?	**Pode vacinar-me contra . . .?** pod vaseeNAR-mə KONtra
I'm on the pill.	**Eu estou a tomar a pílula.** Eoo shtoh a toMAR a PEElola
I take pills for. . . .	**Eu estou a tomar comprimidos para. . . .** Eoo shtoh a toMAR kompreeMEEdoosh PAra
I've lost my. . . .	**Eu perdí. . . .** Eoo pairDEE
–pills.	**–os meus comprimidos.** –oosh MEoosh kompreeMEEdoosh
–prescription.	**–a receita.** –a reSAYta
–glasses.	**–os óculos.** –oosh Okooloosh
I'm allergic to. . . .	**Eu sou alérgico a. . . .** Eoo soh aLAIRzheekoo a
I'm pregnant.	**Estou grávida.** shtoh GRAveeda
I'm a diabetic.	**Sou diabético.** soh deeaBAYteekoo
I'm asthmatic.	**Sou asmático.** soh azhMAteekoo

I'm an epileptic.	**Sou epiléptico.**
	soh epeeLEPteekoo
I have a heart condition.	**Sofro do coração.**
	SOFroo doo kooraSOWNG
I'm worried about my baby.	**Estou preocupada com o meu bébé.**
	shtoh preokooPAda kong oo MEoo beBAY
He won't eat.	**Ele não come.**
	Elə nowng KOmə
He can't swallow.	**Ele não consegue engolir.**
	Elə nowng konSEG eengoLEER

At the dentist's

My tooth aches (very badly).	**Estou com uma dor de dentes (muito grande).**
	shtoh kong OOma door də dentsh (MWEENtoo grand)
A filling has come out.	**Caiu a obturação do dente.**
	ky-Yoo a otooraSOWNG doo dent
–broken.	**–partiu-se a**
	–partYOO-sə a
My tooth has broken.	**Parti um dente.**
	parTEE oong dent
My gums are very sore.	**Tenho as gengivas muito inflamadas.**
	TENyoo ash zhenZHEEvash MWEENtoo eenflaMAdash
–bleeding.	**–a sangrar**
	–a sanGRAR

Entertainment

While you're in Portugal make sure you go to a **Casa de Fado**
This is a restaurant where you can eat and drink late and listen
to the **Fado**, the traditional Portuguese song. It is very expressive
and melancholic, usually sung by a female singer, a **fadista**, and
the whole presentation can be quite dramatic. Probably the best
casas de fado are to be found in the old quarter of Lisbon, the
Bairro Alto.

Bullfighting (**Tourada**) is another typical Portuguese attraction.
It is very different from the Spanish bullfight in that it is more of a
spectacle, a show. The bullfighter is expected to show great skill
and courage but the bull is not allowed to be killed. The whole is
presented in seventeenth-century style. The bullfighting season is
from Easter to October.

General

Is there . . . anywhere?	**Há cá . . .?**
	a ka
–a discothèque	**–alguma discoteca**
	–alGOOma deeshkooTEKa
–a night-club	**–alguma boite/cabaret**
	–alGOOma bwat/kabaRAY
–a jazz-club	**–algum clube de jazz**
	–alGOONG kloob də 'jazz'
–a casino	**–algum casino**
	–alGOONG kaZEEno
–a zoo	**–algum jardim zoológico**
	–alGOONG zharDEENG zo-oLOzheekoo
–a playground	**–algum recreio para as crianças**
	–alGOONG heKRAYoo PAra əsh kreeANsəsh

–a circus	**–algum circo**
	–alGOONG SEERkoo
–a fair	**–alguma feira**
	–alGOOma FAYra
–a bullfight	**–alguma tourada**
	–alGOOma tohRAda
Where is it?	**Onde é que é?**
	ONDee ay kee ay
Where can I buy tickets?	**Onde é que posso comprar bilhetes?**
	ONDee ay kə POSsoo komPRAR beelYETsh

Cinema/Theatre

Theatre performances and the last film showings begin at about 9.30 p.m.

Have you any tickets for tonight?	**Tem bilhetes para esta noite?**
	tayng beelYETsh PAra ESHta noit
Can I book a ticket for tomorrow?	**Posso reservar um bilhete para amanhã?**
	POSsoo rəzərVAR oong beelYET PAra amanYÃ
What's on. . . .	**O que é que vai. . . .**
	oo kee ay ke vy
–tomorrow?	**–amanhã?**
	–amanYÃ
–on Sunday?	**–no Domingo?**
	–noo doMEENGoo
–next week?	**–na semana que vem?**
	–na seMAna kə vyng
Is it. . . .	**É. . . .**
	ay
–good?	**–bom?**
	–bong

–funny?	**–engraçado?** –eengraSAdoo
–exciting?	**–emocionante?** –eemoosyooNANT
–a musical?	**–um musical?** –oong moozeeKAL
–a comedy?	**–uma comédia?** –OOma kooMAYdya
–a thriller?	**–um policial?** –oong pooleesYAL
Two tickets, please.	**Dois bilhetes por favor.** doish beelYETsh fazh faVOOR
At the back.	**Atrás.** aTRASH
At the side.	**De lado.** də LAdoo
At the front.	**À frente.** a frent
(Not) on the gangway.	**(Sem ser) na coxia.** (sayng sair) na kooSHEEa
In the stalls.	**Na plateia.** na plaTAYa
In the circle.	**No primeiro balcão.** noo preeMAYroo balKOWNG
In the gallery.	**No segundo balcão.** noo səGOONdoo balKOWNG
In the middle.	**No meio.** noo MAYoo
In the no-smoking section.	**Na zona de não fumar.** na ZOHna də nowng fooMAR
What time does . . . start?	**A que horas é que começa . . .?** a kee Orəsh ay kə koMEsa
–the play	**–o teatro?** –oo teeATroo
–the main film	**–o filme principal?** –oo feelm preenseePAL

–the programme	**–o programa?**
	–oo prooGRAma
Have you got any programmes?	**Tem programas?**
	tayng prooGRAmash
May I have a programme, please?	**Dá-me um programa por favor?**
	DAmə oong prooGRAma fazh faVOOR
*I'm sorry, we've sold out.	**Já não temos.**
	zha nowng TAYmoosh

Of course, many of these questions and phrases can be used for other forms of entertainment and spectator sports.

NOTICES

E proibido tirar fotografias	No photographs to be taken
Proibida a entrada a menores de 18 anos/para maiores de 18 anos	No children under 18 admitted

The beach

Is it safe to swim here?
Pode-se nadar aqui?
POD-sə naDAR aKEE

Is it safe to dive here?
Pode-se mergulhar aqui?
POD-sə mərgoolYAR aKEE

Is it safe for children?
É seguro para as crianças aqui?
ay səGOOroo PAra əsh
  kreeANsəsh aKEE

Is there a life-guard?
Há algum nadador-salvador aqui?
ay alGOONG nadaDOR-
  salvaDOR aKEE

*There's a strong current here.
Há uma corrente forte aqui.
a OOma kooHENT fort aKEE

*It can be dangerous.
Pode ser perigoso.
pod-sair pəreeGOHzo

I'd like to hire. . . .
Queria alugar. . . .
kəREEa alooGAR

–a deck-chair.
–uma cadeira de lona.
–OOma kaDAYra də LOHna

–a sunshade.
–um guarda-sol.
–oong gwarda-SOL

–a cabin.
–uma barraca.
–OOma baHAka

–a boat.
–um barco.
–oong BARkoo

–a pedalo.
–uma gaivota.
–OOma gyVOta

–a surf-board.
–uma prancha de surf.
–OOma PRANsha də sərf

–some water-skis.
–uns skis.
–oongsh shkeesh

I'd like to. . . .

                        Eu queria. . . .
                        Eoo kəREEa

–go fishing.

                        –ir pescar.
                        –eer pəshKAR

–go underwater-fishing.

                        –fazer pesca submarina.
                        –faZAIR PESHka
                             soomaREEna

–go water-ski-ing.

                        –fazer ski.
                        –faZAIR shkee

–go surfing.

                        –fazer surf.
                        –faZAIR sərf

For one hour.

                        Durante uma hora.
                        dooRANT OOma Ora

For two hours.

                        Durante duas horas.
                        dooRANT DOOash Orash

For the morning.

                        Durante toda a manhã.
                        dooRANT TOHda a manYÃ

How much is it?

                        Quanto custa.
                        KWANtoo KOOSHta

Per hour?

                        Por hora?
                        poor Ora

Per day?

                        Por dia?
                        poor DEEa

Are there any showers?

                        Há chuveiros?
                        a shooVAYroosh

Where can we buy a drink?

                        Onde é que podemos tomar umas
                             bebidas?
                        ONDee ay kə poDEmoosh
                             toMAR OOmash bəBEEdash

Where can we get something to eat?

                        Onde é que podemos comer
                        qualquer coisa?
                        ONDee ay kə poDEmoosh
                           koKAIR kwalKAIR KOIza

NOTICES

proibido tomar banho	Bathing prohibited
proibido mergulhar	Diving prohibited
praia privativa/particular	Private Beach
praia pública	Public Beach
perigo	Danger

Note: It is not safe to swim when a red flag is flying.

Sightseeing

Most towns and resorts have a tourist information office where English is spoken. Look for the notice 'Turismo'. If you are staying in a large hotel the receptionist should be able to help with information on local places of interest.

Where's the nearest tourist office?	**Onde é a agência de turismo mais próxima?**
	ONDee ay a aZHENSya də tooREESHmoo mysh PROSseema
What do you recommend me to visit?	**O que é que me aconselha visitar?**
	oo kee ay kə mə akonSELya veezeeTAR
Where is it?	**Onde é?**
	ONDee ay
Is there anything of interest here?	**Há alguma coisa interessante aqui?**
	a alGOOma KOIza eentərəSANT aKEE
Which is the most interesting....	**Qual é . . . mais interessante?**
	kwal ay . . . mysh eentərəSANT
–museum?	**–o museu**
	–oo mooZEoo

–church?	–a igreja
	–a eeGRAYzha
–district?	–o bairro
	–oo BYhoo
Where is. . . .	Onde é. . . .
	ONDee ay
–the cathedral?	–a catedral?
	–a kateDRAL
–the museum?	–o museu?
	–oo mooZEoo
–the art museum?	–o museu de arte?
	–oo mooZEoo de art
–the castle?	–o castelo?
	–oo kashTEloo
–the old part of town?	–a parte antiga da cidade?
	–a part anTEEga da seeDAD
Is there a coach tour of the town?	Há alguma excursão de camioneta pela cidade?
	a alGOOma shkoorSOWNG de kamyoNET PEla seeDAD
Can one take a boat trip on the river?	Pode-se dar passeios de barco no rio?
	POD-se dar paSAYoosh de BARkoo noo HEEoo
Where does it leave from?	De onde é que partem?
	de ONDee ay ke PARtayng
How much does it cost?	Quanto custa?
	KWANtoo KOOSHta
What time does it leave?	A que horas é que partem?
	a kee Oresh ay ke PARtayng
What time does it get back?	A que horas é que acaba?
	a kee Oresh ay kee aKAba
Is there an open market?	Há alguma feira?
	a alGOOma FAYra
Is there a market every day?	O mercado está aberto todos os dias?

oo mərKAdoo shta aBAIRtoo
TOHdoosh oosh DEEash

Is there a guide?
Há algum guia?
a alGOONG GEEa

Have you got a guide-book?
Tem um guia (livro)?
tayng oong GEEa
(LEEvroo)

In English, please.
Em Inglês por favor.
ayng eenGLAYSH poor faVOOR

Is there a reduction for students?
Fazem desconto para estudantes?
FAZHayng dəshKONtoo PAra
shtooDANTsh

–children?
–crianças?
–kreeANsəsh

NOTICES
E proibido tirar fotografias   No photographs to be taken

Other leisure activities

Where's the nearest. . . .
Onde é . . . mais próximo?
ONDee ay mysh PROSseemoo

–golf club?
–o clube de golfe
–oo kloob də gohlf

–swimming pool?
–a piscina
–a pəshSEEna

–ice-rink?
–o ringue de patinagem em gêlo
–oo heeng də pateeNAZHayng
ayng ZHEloo

–tennis court?
–o corte de tenis
–oo kort də TENees

–football stadium?
–estádio de football
–oo SHTADyoo də FOOTbol

–sailing club?
–o clube de vela náutico
–oo kloob də VEla/NAooteekoo

Does one have to be a member?
E preciso ser-se sócio?
ay prəSEEzoo SAIR-sə SOsyoo

How much does it cost to join?
Quanto custa a inscrição?
KWANtoo KOOSHta a
eenshkreeSOWNG

I'd like to hire. . . .
Eu queria alugar. . . .
Eoo kəREEa alooGAR

I'd like to take lessons.
Eu queria ter umas lições.
Eoo kəREEa tair OOmash
leeSOengsh

I'm a beginner.
Sou um principiante.
son oong preenseepYANT

Can I fish here?
Posso pescar aqui?
POSSoo pəshKAR aKEE

Where can one fish?
Onde é que se pode pescar?
ONDee ay kə se pod pəshKAR

Must I get a permit?
É preciso ter uma licença?
ay prəSEEzoo tair OOma
leeSENsa

Is it an outdoor pool?
É uma piscina ao ar livre?
ay OOma pəshSEEna Aoo ar
LEEvrə

Is it an indoor pool?
É uma piscina coberta?
ay OOma pəshSEEna kooBAIRta

Is it heated?
É aquecida?
ay akeSEEda

Loss or Theft

If you lose something or have something stolen you should inform the hotel, if you're staying in one, or the guardian at the camp or caravan site. The police should also be informed immediately.

Note: If you lose your passport you should contact the nearest consulate at once.

Someone has stolen my. . . .	**Roubaram-me. . . .**
	rohBARowng-mə
I've lost my. . . .	**Perdi. . . .**
	pairDEE
–passport.	**–o meu passaporte.**
	–oo MEoo pasaPORT
–driving licence.	**–a minha carta de condução.**
	–a MEENya KARta də kondooSOWNG
–insurance certificate.	**–o meu certificado de seguro.**
	–oo MEoo sərteefeeKAdoo də səGOOroo
–car keys.	**–as chaves do carro.**
	–ash SHAvəsh doo KAhoo
–log book.	**–o livrete do carro.**
	–oo leeVRET doo KAhoo
–money.	**–o dinheiro.**
	–oo deenYAIRoo
–traveller's cheques.	**–os cheques de viagem.**
	–oosh SHEkəsh də veeAZHayng
–credit cards.	**–os cartões de crédito.**
	–oosh karTOengsh də KREdeetoo
–plane ticket.	**–o bilhete de avião.**
	–oo beelYET də avYOWNG

*When/Where did you lose it?
Quando/Onde é que perdeu?
KWANdoo/ONDee ay kə
pairDEoo

My . . . has disappeared.
Desapareceu. . . .
dəzaparəSEoo

–camera
–a minha máquina fotográfia.
–a MEENya MAkeena foto-
GRAfeeko

–wallet
–a minha carteira.
–a MEENya karTAYra

–handbag
–a minha mala de mão.
–a MEENya MAla də mowng

–briefcase
–a minha pasta.
–a MEENya PASHta

–jewellery
–desapareceram as minhas joias.
–dəzaparəSAIRowng ash
MEENyash ZHOIəsh

*When did you last have it?
Quando foi a última vez que a viu?
KWANdoo foi a OOLteema
vaysh kə a vyoo

It was in my. . . .
Foi. . . .
foi

–car.
–no meu carro.
–noo MEoo KAhoo

–room.
–no meu quarto.
–noo MEoo KWARtoo

–beach-cabin.
–dentro da barraca da praia.
–DENTroo da baHAka da PRYa

Reference Section

Numbers

¼	um quarto oong KWARtoo	22	vinte e dois veent ee DOISH
½	um meio oong MAYoo	30	trinta TREENta
⅓	um terço oong TAIRsoo	40	quarenta kwaRENta
0	zero ZEroo	50	cinquenta seenKWENta
1	um oong	60	sessenta səSENta
2	dois doish	70	setenta səTENta
3	três traysh	80	oitenta oiTENta
4	quatro KWATroo	90	noventa nooVENta
5	cinco SEENkoo	100	cem sayng
6	seis saysh	200	duzentos dooZENtoosh
7	sete set	300	trezentos trəZENtoosh
8	oito OIToo	400	quatrocentos kwatrooSENtoosh
9	nove nov	500	quinhentos keenYENtoosh
10	dez daysh	600	seiscentos sayshSENtoosh
11	onze onz	700	setecentos setSENtoosh
12	doze dohz	800	oitocentos oitSENtoosh
13	treze trez	900	novecentos novSENtoosh
14	catorze kaTOORZ	1,000	mil meel
15	quinze keenz	2,000	dois mil doish meel
16	dezasseis dəzaSAYSH	1,000,000	um milhão oong meelYOWNG
17	dezassete dəzaSET		
18	dezoito dəZOIT		
19	dezanove dəzaNOV		
20	vinte veent		
21	vinte e um veent ee OONG		

Combinations of numbers are formed thus:

131	**cento e trinta e um**
	SENtoo ee TREENta ee oong
372	**trezentos e sententa e dois**
	trəZENtoosh ee səTENta ee doish
1,250	**mil duzentos e cinquenta**
	meel dooZENtoosh ee seenKWENta

Numerical expressions

three-quarters	**três quartos**	traysh KWARtoosh
two thirds	**dois terços**	doish TAIRsoosh
a lot	**muitos**	MWEENtoosh
a little	**poucos**	POHkoosh
a few	**uns poucos**	oongsh POHkoosh
more	**mais**	mysh
less	**menos**	MEnoosh
double	**a dobro**	oo DOHbroo
half	**metade**	meTAD
once	**uma vez**	OOma vaysh
twice	**duas vezes**	DOOash VEZəsh
three times	**três vezes**	traysh VEZəsh
millions of. . . .	**um milhão de. . . .**	oong meelYOWNG də
countless	**sem conta**	sayng KONta

Cardinal numbers

first	**primeiro**	preeMAYroo
second	**segundo**	səGOONdoo
third	**terceiro**	tərSAIRoo
fourth	**quarto**	KWARtoo
fifth	**quinto**	KEENtoo
sixth	**sexto**	SAYSHtoo
seventh	**sétimo**	SETeemoo
eighth	**oitavo**	oiTAvoo
ninth	**nono**	NOHnoo
tenth	**décimo**	DEseemoo

The time

Excuse me.	**Faz favor.** fazh faVOOR
What's the time, please?	**Que horas são, faz favor?** kee Orash sowng, fazh faVOOR
It's one o'clock (exactly).	**É uma hora (em ponto).** ay OOma Ora (ayng PONtoo)
It's (nearly) two o'clock.	**São (quase) duas horas.** sowng KWAzee DOOash Orash
It's (just after) three o'clock.	**São (. . . pouco passa das) três horas.** sowng (POHkoo PASSa dash) traysh Orash
It's . . . past three.	**São três e. . . .** sowng traysh ee
–a quarter	**–um quarto.** –oong KWARtoo
–half	**–meia.** –MAYa
–ten minutes	**–dez.** –dezh
It's . . . to four.	**São . . . para as quatro.** sowng PArash KWATroo
–a quarter	**–um quarto** –oong KWARtoo
–twenty minutes	**–vinte** –veent
At two o'clock.	**Às duas horas.** ash DOOash Orash
It's midday.	**É meio dia.** ay MAYoo DEEa
It's midnight.	**É meia noite.** ay MAYa noit

Some time phrases

At night	**À noite**	
	a noit	
In the morning	**De manhã**	
	də manYÃ	
–afternoon	**–de tarde**	
	–də tard	
–evening	**–de tarde**	
	–də tard	
At midday	**Ào meio dia**	
	Aoo MAYoo DEEa	
At midnight	**À meia noite**	
	a MAYa noit	
Today	**Hoje**	
	ohzh	
Tomorrow	**Amanhã**	
	amanYÃ	
Tonight	**Esta noite**	
	ESHta noit	
Last week	**A semana passada**	
	a səMAna paSAda	
–month	**–o mês passado**	
	–oo maysh paSAdoo	
–year	**–o ano passado**	
	–oo Anoo paSAdoo	
Next week	**Para a semana que vem**	
	PAra a səMAna kə vyng	
–month	**–para o mês que vem**	
	–PAra oo maysh kə vyng	
The day after tomorrow	**Depois de amanhã**	
	də POISH də amanYÃ	
Yesterday	**Ontem**	
	ONtayng	
The day before yesterday	**Antes de ontem**	
	ANTəsh də ONtayng	
This morning	**Esta manhã**	
	ESHta manYÃ	

This afternoon	**Esta tarde** ESHta tard
This evening	**Esta noite** ESHta noit
I'm sorry I'm late.	**Desculpe o meu atraso.** dəshKOOP oo MEoo aTRASsoo
I'm afraid I'm early.	**Parece-me que vim cedo demais.** pəREsəmə kəveeng SEdoo dəMYSH
See you later.	**Até logo.** aTAY LOgoo
See you tomorrow.	**Até amanhã.** aTAY amanYÃ
Now	**Agora** aGOORa
Soon	**De aqui a um bocado** də aKEE a oong booKAdoo
As soon as possible	**Logo que possa** LOgoo kə POSsa
One day	**Um dia** oong DEEa
The other day	**No outro dia** noo OHtroo DEEa
In a minute	**Num minuto** noong meeNOOtoo
In a few minutes	**De aqui a uns minutos** də aKEE a oonsh meeNOOtoosh
Earlier	**Mais cedo** mysh SEdoo
Later	**Mais tarde** mysh tard
In a week's time	**De aqui a uma semana** də aKEE a OOma səMAna
In a month's time	**De aqui a um mês** də aKEE a oong maysh
Wait a minute	**Espere um minuto** shpair oong meeNOOtoo

The seasons

Spring	**Primavera**	preemaVAIRa
Summer	**Verão**	vəROWNG
Autumn	**Outono**	ohTOHnoo
Winter	**Inverno**	eenVAIRnoo

In spring — **Na primavera**   na preemaVAIRa

During the winter — **Durante o inverno**   dooRANT oo eenVAIRnoo

In summer — **No verão**   noo vəROWNG

A summer dress — **Um vestido de verão**   oong veshTEEdoo də vəROWNG

A winter holiday — **Umas férias de inverno**   OOmash FAYryash də eenVAIRnoo

Winter sports — **Desportos de inverno**   dəshPORtoosh də eenVAIRnoo

Days of the week

Monday	**Segunda-feira**	səGOONda FAYra
Tuesday	**Terça-feira**	TAIRsa FAYra
Wednesday	**Quarta-feira**	KWARta FAYra
Thursday	**Quinta-feira**	KEENta FAYra
Friday	**Sexta-feira**	SAYSHta FAYra
Saturday	**Sábado**	SAbadoo
Sunday	**Domingo**	dooMEENgoo

on Monday — **na segunda-feira**
na səGOONda FAYra

every Saturday — **todos os sábados**
TOHdoosh oosh SAbadoosh

last Tuesday — **na terça-feira passada**
na TAIRsa FAYra paSAda

next Friday — **na próxima sexta-feira**
na PROSseema SAYSHta FAYra

a week next Friday — **de sexta a oito dias**
də SAYSHta a OItoo DEEash

a week last Sunday	**fez uma semana no domingo passado**
	fezh OOma səMAna noo dooMEENgoo paSAdoo
except Sundays	**excepto aos domingos**
	eeshSEToo Aoosh dooMEENgoosh
every other day	**todos os outros dias**
	TOHdoosh oosh OHtroosh DEEash
a fortnight	**duas semanas/quinze dias**
	DOOash səMAnash/keenz DEEash
a month	**um mês**
	oong maysh
a year	**um ano**
	oong Anoo

The months

January	**Janeiro**	zhaNAYroo
February	**Fevereiro**	fəvəRAYroo
March	**Março**	MARsoo
April	**Abril**	aBREEL
May	**Maio**	MYoo
June	**Junho**	ZHOONyoo
July	**Julho**	ZHOOLyoo
August	**Agosto**	aGOSHtoo
September	**Setembro**	səTEMbroo
October	**Outubro**	ohTOObroo
November	**Novembro**	nooVEMbroo
December	**Dezembro**	dəZEMbroo

in May	**em Maio**
	ayng MYoo
next March	**no próximo mês de Março**
	noo PROSseemoo maysh də MARsoo
last June	**no passado mês de Junho**
	noo paSAdoo maysh də ZHOONyoo
at the beginning of April	**no principio do mês de Abril**
	noo preenSEEpyoo doo maysh də aBREEL

at the end of July   nos fins de Julho
                            noosh feensh də ZHOOLyoo

Colours

beige	**beije**	bayzh
black	**preto**	PREtoo
blue	**azul**	aZOOL
brown	**castanho**	kashTANyoo
cream	**creme**	krem
crimson	**carmesim**	karməZEENG
gold	**dourado**	dohRAdoo
grey	**cinzento**	seenZENtoo
green	**verde**	vaird
orange	**côr de laranja**	kohr də laRANzha
pink	**côr de rosa**	kohr də ROza
purple	**roxo**	ROHshoo
red	**vermelho**	vərMELyoo
scarlet	**escarlate**	əshkarLAT
silver	**prateado**	pratYAdoo
white	**branco**	BRANkoo
yellow	**amarelo**	amaRELoo
dark (brown)	**(castanho) escuro**	(kashTANyoo) əshKOOroo
light (blue)	**(azul) claro**	(aZOOL) KLARoo
bright (red)	**(vermelho) vivo**	(vərMELyoo) VEEvoo

Countries

I come from. . . .	Eu sou. . . .	Eoo soh
Australia	**da Austrália**	da AooSHTRALya
Austria	**da Austria**	da Aooshtrya
Brazil	**do Brasil**	doo braZEEL
Canada	**do Canadá**	doo kanaDA
England	**de Inglaterra**	də eenglaTEha
France	**de França**	də FRANsa
Germany	**da Alemanha**	da aləMANya

Greece	**da Grécia** da GREsya
Holland	**da Holanda** da oLANda
India	**da India** da EENDya
Ireland	**da Irlanda** da eerLANda
Italy	**da Itália** da eeTALya
Japan	**do Japão** doo zhaPOWNG
Mexico	**do México** doo MESHeekoo
New Zealand	**da Nova Zelândia** da NOHva zəLANDya
Pakistan	**do Paquistão** doo pakeeSHTOWNG
Peru	**do Perú** doo peROO
Portugal	**de Portugal** də poortooGAL
Scotland	**da Escócia** da esKOSya
South Africa	**da África do Sul** da AFreeka doo sool
Spain	**de Espanha** də SHPANya
The USA	**dos Estados Unidos da América** doosh əshTAdoosh ooNEEdoosh da aMAYreeka
Wales	**do País de Gales** doo paEESH də GALəsh

Nationalities

I'm....	**Eu sou....** Eoo soh
an Arab	**árabe** ARab
Australian	**Australiano** AooshtralYAnoo
Austrian	**Austríaco** AooshTREEako
Brazilian	**Brasileiro** brazeeLAYroo
Canadian	**Canadiano** kanadYAAnoo
French	**Francês** franSAYSH
German	**Alemão** aləMOWNG
Greek	**Grego** GREgoo
English	**Inglês** eenGLAYSH
Dutch	**Holandês** olanDAYSH
Indian	**Indiano** eendYAnoo
Irish	**Irlandês** eerlanDAYSH
Israeli	**Israelita** eeshraeeLEEta
Italian	**Italiano** eetalYAnoo
Japanese	**Japonês** zhapoNAYSH

Mexican	**Mexicano** məsheeKAnoo
a New Zealander	**Novo Zelandês** NOHvoo zəlanDAYSH
Pakistani	**Paquistanês** pakeeshtaNAYSH
Peruvian	**Peruano** perooAnoo
Portuguese	**Português** poortooGAYSH
Scottish	**Escocês** əshkooSAYSH
South African	**Sul Africano** sool afreeKAnoo
Spanish	**Espanhol** əshpanYOL
North American	**Norte Americano** nort aməreeeKAnoo
Welsh	**Galês** gaLAYSH

Public holidays in Portugal

January 1st
Shrove Tuesday
Good Friday
April 25th ('Revolution' day)
June 10th (National Day)
Whitsun August 15th (Assumption)
Corpus Christi October 5th (Proclamation of the Republic)
November 1st (All Saints' Day)
December 1st (Restoration of Independence)
December 8th (Immaculate Conception)
December 25th

There is also a local holiday on the saint's day of the town or province,
(*e.g.* June 13th, St. Anthony, in Lisbon).

Brazil has fewer holidays:
January 1st
Good Friday
April 21st (Brazil's Independence Day)
September 7th (Independence Day)
November 1st (All Saint's Day)
December 25th
and the famous four days before Ash Wednesday, Carnaval

Useful notices

Entrada	Entrance
Saída	Exit
Proibida a entrada	No entrance
Aberto	Open
Fechado	Closed
Senhoras	Ladies' toilet
Homens/Cavalheiros	Gentlemen's toilet
Perigo	Danger
Proibido	Forbidden
Proibido fumar	No smoking
Privado	Private
Turismo	Tourist Information Office

CONVERSION TABLES

YARDS TO METRES

yd	yd *or* m	m
1.094	1	0.914
2.187	2	1.829
3.281	3	2.743
4.374	4	3.658
5.468	5	4.572
6.562	6	5.486
7.655	7	6.401
8.749	8	7.315
9.843	9	8.230
10.936	10	9.144
21.872	20	18.288
27.340	25	22.860
54.681	50	45.720
109.361	100	91.439
546.805	500	457.195

INCHES TO CENTIMETRES

in	in *or* cm	cm
0.394	1	2.540
0.787	2	5.080
1.181	3	7.620
1.575	4	10.160
1.169	5	12.700
2.362	6	15.240
2.756	7	17.780
3.150	8	20.320
3.543	9	22.860
3.937	10	25.400
7.874	20	50.800
9.843	25	63.500
19.685	50	127.000
39.370	100	254.000

MILES TO KILOMETRES

miles	miles or km	km
0.621	1	1.609
1.242	2	3.218
1.864	3	4.827
2.485	4	6.437
3.107	5	8.046
3.728	6	9.655
4.350	7	11.265
4.971	8	12.874
5.592	9	14.483
6.214	10	16.093
15.535	25	40.232
31.070	50	80.465
46.605	75	120.696
62.136	100	160.930
124.272	200	321.860
186.408	300	382.790
310.680	500	804.650

GALLONS TO LITRES

gal	l or gal	l
0.22	1	4.55
0.44	2	9.09
0.66	3	13.64
0.88	4	18.18
1.10	5	22.73
1.32	6	27.28
1.54	7	31.83
1.76	8	36.37
1.98	9	40.91
2.20	10	45.46
4.40	20	90.92
6.60	30	136.38
8.80	40	181.84
11.00	50	227.30
16.50	75	340.95
22.00	100	454.59
33.00	150	681.89

POUNDS TO KILOGRAMMES

lb	lb or kg	kg
2.205	1	0.453
4.409	2	0.907
6.614	3	1.360
8.818	4	1.814
11.023	5	2.268
13.228	6	2.721
15.432	7	3.175
17.637	8	3.628
19.841	9	4.082
22.046	10	4.435
44.092	20	9.071
55.116	25	11.339
110.232	50	22.680
220.464	100	45.359

POUNDS PER SQUARE INCH TO KILOGRAMMES PER SQUARE CENTIMETRE

lb/in²	kg/cm²
18	1.266
20	1.406
22	1.547
25	1.758
29	2.039
32	2.250
35	2.461
36	2.531
39	2.742
40	2.812

TEMPERATURE:
FAHRENHEIT AND CENTIGRADE

°F	°C	
−22	−30	
−4	−20	
+14	−10	
+23	−5	
+32	0	
+41	+5	
+50	+10	
+68	+20	
+86	+30	normal
+98.4	+36.9	body
+104	+40	temperature
+122	+50	
+140	+60	
+157	+70	
+176	+80	
+194	+90	
+212	+100	

SIZE CONVERSION TABLES

This is only a general guide. and it is always advisable to try on clothes etc. before buying them.

Women's clothes

	ENGLISH	PORTUGUESE		ENGLISH	PORTUGUESE
Dresses	32	38	Hats	$6\frac{1}{8}$	50 cm
	34	40		$6\frac{1}{4}$	51
	36	42		$6\frac{3}{8}$	52
	38	44		$6\frac{1}{2}$	53
	40	46		$6\frac{5}{8}$	54
	42	48		$6\frac{3}{4}$	55
				$6\frac{7}{8}$	56
Blouses	30	42		7	57
	32	44		$7\frac{1}{8}$	58
	34	46		$7\frac{1}{4}$	59
	36	48		$7\frac{3}{8}$	60
	38	50		$7\frac{1}{2}$	61
	40	52			
	42	54	Shoes	2	34
				$2\frac{1}{2}$	35
Sweaters	32	42		3	$35\frac{1}{2}$
	34	44		$3\frac{1}{2}$	36
	36	46		4	$36\frac{1}{2}$
	38	48		$4\frac{1}{2}$	$37\frac{1}{2}$
	40	50		5	38
				$5\frac{1}{2}$	$38\frac{1}{2}$
Stockings	8	0		6	$39\frac{1}{4}$
	$8\frac{1}{2}$	1		$6\frac{1}{2}$	40
	9	2		7	$40\frac{1}{2}$
	$9\frac{1}{2}$	3		$7\frac{1}{2}$	41
	10	4		8	42
	$10\frac{1}{2}$	5			
	11	6			

Vocabulary

The following alphabetical list of English words and their equivalent Portuguese meanings and pronunciation is based on the words used in this phrasebook. For example, the word 'connection' is given only in its meaning of a train connection, and this is indicated, where possible, in the list. For a comprehensive list of Portuguese words a pocket dictionary is recommended.

As the Reference Section at the end of the phrasebook contains lists of the numbers, days of the week, months, countries and nationalities these will not be included in the Vocabulary List.

For the key to the 'phonetic' transcription, look at the Pronunciation Guide on page 4.

a	**um/uma**	oong/OOma
(to be) able to	**poder**	pooDAIR
above	**acima**	aSEEma
about	**acerca**	aSAIRka
accelerator	**acelerador**	aseləraDOOR
ache	**dor**	door
aeroplane	**avião**	avYOWNG
aerogramme	**aerograma**	a-airoGRAma
(I'm) afraid (sorry)	**estou a ver que....**	shtoh a vair kə
after	**depois**	dePOISH
afternoon	**tarde**	tard
aftershave	**loção de barba**	looSOWNG də BARba
again	**outra vez**	OHtra vaysh
against	**contra**	KONtra
ago	**há....**	a
air-conditioning	**ar condicionado**	ar koondeesyoNAdoo
air mail	**correio aéreo**	koHAYoo aAIRyoo

all	tudo	TOOdoo
all right	está bem	shta bayng
allergic	alérgico	aLAIRzheekoo
ambulance	ambulância	ambooLANSya
and	e	ee
ankle	tornozelo	toornooZEloo
another	outro	OHtroo
antiseptic cream	creme antiséptico	krem anteeSEPteekoo
any	qualquer	kwalKAIR
anyone	qualquer um	kwalkair oong
anything	qualquer coisa	kwalkair KOIza
apple	maçã	maSÃ
appointment	entrevista/consulta (if medical)	entreVEESHta/ koonSOOLta
apricot	damasco	daMASHkoo
arm	braço	BRAsoo
around	em volta (de)	ayng VOLta (də)
(to) arrive	chegar	shəGAR
arrivals	chegada	shəGAda
art museum	museu de arte	mooZEoo də art
as	como	KOmoo
ashtray	cinzeiro	seenZAIRoo
ask	perguntar	pərgoonTAR
asthmatic	asmático	ashMAteekoo
at	em	ayng
automatic	automático	owtooMAteekoo
autumn	outono	ohTOnoo
baby	bébé	beBAY
a back	costas	KOSHtash
bad	mau	MAoo
bags (suitcases)	malas	MAlash
baked	cozido no forno	kooZEEdoo noo FOORnoo
baker's	padaria	padaREEa
banana	banana	baNAna

bandage	ligadura	leegaDOOra
bar	bar	bar
barber	barbeiro	barBAYroo
bath	banho	BANyoo
bathing	banho	BANyoo
bathroom	casa de banho	KAza də BANyoo
battery	bateria	batəREEa
(to) be	estar/ser	shtar/sair
beach	praia	PRYa
beach cabin	barraca	baHAka
beach shoes	sapatos de praia	saPAtoosh də PRYa
beach sandals	sandálias de praia	sanDALyash də PRYa
beans	feijões	fayZHOengsh
beautiful	bonito	booNEEtoo
because	porque	POORk
bed	cama	KAma
bedroom	quarto de cama	KWARtoo də KAma
beef	carne de vaca	karn də VAka
beer	cerveja	sərVEzha
before	antes de	ANTəsh də
(to) begin	começar	koomə SAR
beginning	princípio	preenSEEPyoo
beginner	principiante	preenseepYANT
behind	atrás de	aTRASH də
beige	beige	bayzh
berth	beliche	bəLEESH
better	melhor	məlYOR
between	entre	entrə
bicycle	bicicleta	beeseeKLEta
big	grande	grand
bikini	bikini	beeKEEnee
biro	esferográfica	shferooGRAfeeka
black	preto	PREtoo
blanket	cobertor	koobərTOOR
bleed	sangrar	sanGRAR
bleeding	a sangrar	a sanGRAR
blocked	bloqueado	blookeAdoo

blouse	blusa	BLOOza
blow-dried	'Brushing'	brushing
blue	azul	aZOOL
board (full)	pensão completa	pənSOWNG koomPLEta
board (half)	meia pensão	MAYa pənSOWNG
boat	barco	BARkoo
boiled	cozido	kooZEEdoo
book	livro	LEEvroo
(to) book	reservar	rəzərVAR
boots	botas	BOtash
bottle	garrafa	gaHAfa
bottle-opener	saca-rolhas (cork)/ abre-garrafas	SAka-ROOLyash/Abrə- gaHAfash
boy-friend	amigo	aMEEgoo
bra	soutien	sootYANG
braised	guisado	geeZAdoo
brake	travão	traVOWNG
brake-fluid	óleo do travão	OHleoo doo traVOWNG
brake-light	luzes do travão	LOOzəsh doo traVOWNG
brandy	aguardente	agwarDENT
bread	pão	powng
breakfast	pequeno almoço	peKAYnoo alMOSsoo
brief-case	pasta	PASHta
bright	brilhante	breelYANT
(to) bring	trazer	traZAIR
broken	partido	parTEEdoo
broken down	estragado	shtraGAdoo
brother	irmão	eerMOWNG
brown	castanho	kashTANyoo
buffet-car	carruagem bufete	kahooAzhayng booFET
bulb (light)	lampada	LAMpada
bus	autocarro	owtooKAhoo
bus-stop	paragem do autocarro	paRAzhayng doo owtooKAhoo
butcher's	talho	TALyoo
butter	manteiga	manTAYga
(to) buy	comprar	koomPRAR

cabbage	couve	kohv
cabin	barraca	baHAka
(to) cable	telegrafar	telegraFAR
café	café	kaFAY
(to) call (phone)	telefonar	telefoNAR
a call	um telefonema	oong telefoNEma
camera	máquina fotográfica	MAkeena fotoGRAfeeka
camping	acampamento	akampaMENtoo
camping-gas	gas para campismo	gash PAra kamPEEZHmoo
camping supplies shop	lojas de campismo	LOZHash de kamPEEZHmoo
campsite	parque de campismo	park de kamPEEZHmoo
can (tin)	lata	LAta
can (to be able)	poder	pooDAIR
cap	boné	boNAY
car	carro	KAhoo
car park	parque de estacionamento	park de shtasyonaMENtoo
car wash	lavagem automática	laVAzhayng owtooMAteekoo
carafe	garrafa para água	gaHAfa PAra AGwa
caravan	caravana	karaVAna
caravan site	parque de campismo	park de kamPEEZHmoo
carburettor	carburador	karbooraDOOR
cardigan	casaco de lã	kaZAkoo de la(ng)
careful	cuidadoso	kweedaDOzoo
carrots	cenouras	seNOHrash
(to) carry on	continuar	koonteenooAR
cash	pronto pagamento	PRONtoo pagaMENtoo
(to) cash	converter em dinheiro	konverTAIR ayng deeNAYroo
casino	casino	kaZEEnoo
(cathedral) castle	(catedral) castelo	(kateDRAL) kashTEloo
centre	centro	SENtroo
certificate	certificado	serteefeeKAdoo
change (money)	trôco	TROHkoo
(to) change	trocar	trooKAR

charge	preço	PREsoo
chauffeur-driven	(carro) com motorista	kong mootooREESHta
cheap	barato	baRAtoo
cheese	queijo	KAYzhoo
(to) check in (hotels)	check in	Check in
chemist	farmácia	farMASya
cheque	cheque	sheck
chewing-gum	pastilha elástica	pashTEELya LASHteeka
child	criança	kreeANsa
children	crianças	kreeANsash
chocolate	chocolate	shokoLAT
chop (cutlet)	costeleta	kooshtəLEta
church	igreja	eeGRAYzha
cigarette	cigarro	seeGAhoo
cigarillos	cigarrilhas	seegaHEELyoo
cinema	cinema	SEEnəma
circle	balcão	balKOWNG
circus	circo	SEERkoo
class	classe	klas
clean	limpo	LEEMpoo
(to) clean	limpar	leemPAR
clever	esperto	SHPAIRtoo
closed	fechado	fəSHAdoo
clothes	roupas	ROHpash
clothes shop	loja de roupa	LOzha de ROHpa
clutch (car)	embraiagem	eembry-YAzhayng
coach	camioneta	kamyoNETa
coat	casaco	kaZAkoo
cod	bacalhau	bakalYAoo
coffee	café	kaFAY
a cold	constipação	koonshteepaSOWNG
cold	frio	FREEoo
colour	côr	kohr
colour print	impressão a côres	eemprəSOWNG a KOHRəsh

colour slide	slide a côres	'slide' a KOHRəsh
(to) come	vir	veer
comedy	comédia	kooMAYDya
compartment	compartimento	koomparteeMENtoo
comprehensive	compreensivo	koompre-enSEEvoo
condition	condição	koondeeSOWNG
conditioner	condicionador	koondeesyonaDOOR
connection (train)	transbordo	trashBORdoo
constipation	prisão de ventre	preeZOWNG də VENTrə
convertible	un carro descapotável	oong KAhoo dəshkapoTAvel
cooked	cozinhado	koozeenYAdoo
corduroy	belbutina	bəlbooTEEna
(to) cost	custar	kooshTAR
cot	cama	KAma
cotton	algodão	algooDOWNG
cotton-wool	algodão em rama	algooDOWNG ayng RAma
cough	tosse	toss
cough medicine	remédio para a tosse	rəMAYDyoo PAra a toss
counter	balcão	balKOWNG
countless	sem conta	sayng KONta
cramp	caímbra	kaYEEMbra
cravat	gravata	graVAta
cream (colour)	creme	krem
cream	creme	krem
credit card	cartão de crédito	karTOWNG də KRAYdeetoo
crepe bandage	ligadura de crepe	leegaDOOra də krep
crimson	carmezim	karməZEENG
(to) cross	atravessar	atraveSAR
cross-roads	cruzamento	kroozaMENtoo
cup	chávena	SHAvəna
current	corrente	kooHENT
customs	direitos alfandegários	deeRAYtoosh alfandəGARyoosh

customs declaration form	impresso de declaração alfandegária	eemPRESsoo də dəklaraSOWNG alfandəGARya
(to) cut	cortar	kóorTAR
(to) cut off (phone)	ligação cortada	leegaSOWNG koorTAda
damp	húmido	OOmeedoo
dance	dança	DANsa
danger	perigo	pəREEgoo
dangerous	perigoso	pəreeGOzoo
dark	escuro	SHKOOroo
day	dia	DEEa
(to) declare	declarar	dəklaRAR
deck chair	cadeira de lona	kaDAYra də LOna
delay	demora	deMOra
delivery	entrega	eenTREga
deodorant	desodorizante	dezodoreeZANT
departures	partidas	parTEEdash
deposit	depósito	dəPOZHeetoo
(to) develop (film)	revelar	rəvəLAR
diabetic	diabético	deeaBAYteekoo
different	diferente	deefəRENT
difficult	difícil	deeFEEseel
digestive pills	pastilhas para a digestão	pashTEELyash PAra a deezheSHTOWNG
dinner	jantar	zhanTAR
direct	directo	deeREToo
direct dialling	ligação directa	leegaSOWNG deeRETa
dirty	sujo	SOOzhoo
discothèque	discoteca	deeshkoTEka
district	bairro	BYhoo
(to) dive	mergulhar	mərgoolYAR
dizzy	aturdido	atoorDEEdoo
doctor	médico	MAYdeekoo
down	em baixo	ayng BYshoo
double	duplo	DOOploo
double room	quarto de casal	KWARtoo de kaZAL

dress	vestido	vəshTEEdoo
a drink	uma bebida	OOma bəBEEda
(to) drink	beber	bəBAIR
drinking water	água para beber	Agwa PAra bəBAIR
(to) drive	conduzir	koondooZEER
driving licence	carta de condução	KARta də koondooSOWNG
during	durante	dooRANT
dyed	tingído	teenZHEEdoo
ear	ouvido	ooVEEdoo
ear-ache	dores de ouvido	DOHrəsh də ohVEEdoo
early	cedo	SEdoo
easy	fácil	FAseel
eat	comer	kooMAIR
eggs	ovos	Ovoosh
electrician	electricista	eelektreeSEEshta
electricity	electricidade	eelektreeseeDAD
emergency	emergência	eemərZHAYNSya
empty	vazio	vaZEEoo
(the) end	fim	feeng
engaged (phone)	a falar	a faLAR
English	inglês	eehGLAYSH
enlarge	ampliar	amplYAR
enough	bastante	bashTANT
entry	entrada	eenTRAda
entry (on a bill)	conta	KONta
envelope	sobrescrito	sobrəSHKREEtoo
epileptic	epiléptico	epeeLEPteekoo
evening	noite	noit
exactly	exactamente	eezataMENT
exciting	emocionante	eemosyoNANT
excuse me	desculpe	dəshKOOP
exercise book	caderno de exercícios	kaDAIRnoo dez zərSEESyoosh
expensive	caro	KAroo
exposure (film)	fotografia	fotoograFEEa

express	**expresso**	əshPRESsoo
extension (phone)	**extensão**	shtenSOWNG
extra	**extra**	AYSHtra
face cream	**creme para a cara**	krem PAra a KAra
facing	**em frente**	ayng frent
faint	**desmaiado**	dəzhmyAdo
a fair	**feira**	FAYra
fan-belt	**correia da ventoinha**	koHAYa da ventoEENya
far	**longe**	lonzh
fare	**bilhete**	beelYET
fast	**depressa**	dəPRESsa
(to) feel	**sentir**	sənTEER
fever	**febre**	febr
few	**pouco**	POHkoo
(to) fill	**encher**	eenSHAIR
(to) fill in	**preencher**	pree-enSHAIR
a filling	**obturação**	otooraSOWNG
film (cinema)	**filme**	feelm
film (camera)	**rolo de fotografias**	ROloo də fotograFEEash
fine (weather)	**bom**	bong
fine (well)	**bem**	bayng
first	**primeiro**	preeMAYroo
first aid kit	**estojo de primeiros socorros**	SHTOZHoo də preeMAYroosh sooKOhoosh
fish	**peixe**	paysh
(to) fish	**pescar**	pəshKAR
(to) fit	**provar**	prooVAR
fizzy	**gasoso**	gaZOzoo
flash bulb	**flash**	flash
flat (battery)	**descarregada**	dəshkaheGAda
flight	**vôo**	VOHoo
floor	**chão**	showng
florist	**florista**	flooREEshta
food	**comida**	kooMEEda

food-poisoning	intoxicação	eentosseekaSOWNG
foot	pé	pay
foot-brake	travão de pé	traVOWNG də pay
football stadium	estádio de football	SHTADyoo də FOOTbol
for	por	poor
forbidden	proibido	prooeeBEEdoo
fork	garfo	GARfoo
a form	impresso	eemPRESsoo
fortnight	quinzena	keenZEna
(to) forward	enviar	eenvYAR
forwarding address	endereço	eendəREsoo
fragile	frágil	FRAzheel
fried	frito	FREEtoo
friend	amigo	aMEEgoo
from	de	də
front	frente	frent
fruit	fruta	FROOta
fruit juice	sumo de fruta	SOOmoo də FROOta
full	cheio	SHAYoo
funny	engraçado	eengraSAdoo
fur	pele	pel
gallery	galeria	galəREEa
gangway	passagem	pasSAzhayng
garage	garagem	gaRAzhayng
gargle	gargarejo	gargaREzhoo
gas-light	lampada de gás	LAMpada də gash
gate (airport)	porta	POORta
gears	mudanças	mooDANsash
(to) get off (bus, train)	sair	saEER
girl-friend	amiga	aMEEga
(to) give	dar	dar
glass	copo	KOpoo
glasses	óculos	Okooloosh
glossy	brilhante	breelYANT
(to) go	ir	eer

(to) go out	sair	saEER
gold	ouro	OHroo
golf club	clube de golfe	kloob də GOLf
good	bom	bong
goodbye	adeus	aDEoosh
grapes	uvas	OOvash
grapefruit	toranja	tooRANzha
green	verde	vaird
greengrocer	lugar das hortaliças	looGAR dash ortaLEEsash
grey	cinzento	seenZENtoo
grilled	grelhado	grəlYAdoo
grocer's	mercearia	mərseaREEa
ground floor	rés-do-chão	raysh-doo-SHOWNG
ground-sheet	chão da tenda	showng da TENDa
guide	guia	GEEa
guide-book	guia	GEEa
gums (teeth)	gengivas	zhenZHEEvash
hair	cabelo	kaBEloo
hair-dresser	cabeleireiro	kabələRAYroo
half	metade	məTAD
ham	fiambre	fYAMbr
hand-bag	mala de mão	MAla də MOWNG
hand-brake	travão de mão	traVOWNG də mowng
hat	chapéu	shaPEoo
(to) have	ter	tair
(to) have to	ter de	tair də
head	cabeça	kaBEsa
headlights	faróis	faROISH
heart	coração	kooraSOWNG
heated	aquecido	akəSEEdoo
heating	aquecimento	akəseeMENtoo
heavy	pesado	pəZAdoo
heel	calcanhar	kalkanYAR
hello	olá	oLA
help!	socorro	sooKOhoo

(to) help	ajudar	azhooDAR
here	aqui	aKEE
high	alto	ALtoo
(to) hire	alugar	alooGAR
(to) hold on (phone)	esperar	shpeRAR
home	casa	KAza
husband	marido	maREEdoo
(to) hope	esperar	shpeRAR
horn (car)	buzina	booZEEna
hot	quente	kent
hotel	hotel	oTEL
hour	hora	Ora
how	como	KOmoo
how many	quantos	KWANtoosh
hungry	fome	fohm
a hurry	com pressa	kong PRESsa
hurry!	depressa	dəPRESsa
(to) hurt	ferir	fəREER
ice	gelo	ZHEloo
ice-rink	folha de gelo	FOLya də ZHEloo
ill	doente	dwent
in	em	ayng
into	em	ayng
included	incluído	eenklooEEdoo
indigestion	indigestão	eendeezheshTOWNG
indoor (pool)	coberta	kooBAIRta
infection	infecção	eenfesSOWNG
information	informação	eenfoormaSOWNG
information office	balcão de informações	balKOWNG də eenfoormaSOengsh
(to) inoculate	inocular	eenokooLAR
insurance	seguro	səGOOroo
(to) intend	pretender	prətenDAIR
interesting	interessante	eentərəSANT
international	internacional	eentərnasyoNAL
ironmonger	ferreiro	feHAYroo

jacket	casaco	kaZAkoo
jazz club	clube de jazz	kloob də jazz
a jersey	camisola de lã	kameeZOla də la(ng)
jewellery	joalharia	joalyaREEa
(to) join (club)	fazer-se sócio de	fəZAIR-sə SOHSyoo də
just (only)	só	soh
(to) keep	guardar	gwarDAR
key	chave	shav
kidneys	ríns	reensh
kitchen	cozinha	kooZEENya
knife	faca	FAka
lamb	ovelha	ooVELya
last	último	OOLteemoo
(to) last	durar	dooRAR
late	atrasado	atraZAdoo
(to) launder (lit. wash and iron)	lavar e passar a ferro	laVAR e pasSAR a FEhoo
launderette	lavandaria	lavandaREEa
laundry	lavandaria	lavandaREEa
lavatory	casa de banho	KAza də BANyoo
laxative	laxatívo	laksaTEEvoo
leather	cabedal	kabəDAL
(to) leave	deixar	daySHAR
left	esquerda	SHKAIRda
leg	perna	PAIRna
lemonade	limonada	leemoNAda
less	menos	MENoosh
lesson	lição	leeSOWNG
letter	carta	KARta
lettuce	alface	alFAS
licence	licença	leeSENsa
life-guard	nadador-salvador	nadaDOOR salvaDOOR
lift	elevador	eelevaDOOR
light	leve	lev

a light	luz	loozh
(to) like	gostar (de)	gooshTAR də
like (as)	como, igual	KOmoo eeGWAL
line (underground)	linha	LEENya
linen	linho	LEENyoo
lip-cream	creme para os lábios	KREma PAra oosh LAByoosh
lip-stick	baton	baTONG
litre	litro	LEEtroo
little	pequeno	peKAYnoo
a little	um pouco	oong POHkoo
liver	fígado	FEEgadoo
loaf	um pão	oong powng
local	local	looKAL
lock	fechadura	feshaDOOra
log-book	livrete de carro	leeVRET doo KAhoo
long	comprido	koomPREEdoo
loose	solto	SOLtoo
(to) lose	perder	pərDAIR
lost	perdido	pərDEEdoo
Lost Property (office)	perdidos e achados	pərDEEdoosh ee aSHAdoosh
a lot	muito	MWEENtoo
lounge	sala/salão	SAla/saLOWNG
low	baixo	BYshoo
lovely	agradável	agraDAvel
lozenges	pastilhas	pashTEELyash
luggage	bagagem	baGAzhayng
lunch	almoço	alMOSsoo
(to) make	fazer	fəZAIR
make-up	cosméticos	koozhMEteekoosh
main film	filme principal	feelm preenseePAL
main road	rua principal	ROOa preenseePAL
manager	gerente	zheRENT
map	mapa	MApa

market	mercado	mərKAdoo
matches	fósforos	FOSHfooroosh
matt (finish)	(superfície) mate	soopərFEEsyə mat
may	poder	pooDAIR
me	mim	meeng
(to) mean	quer dizer	kair deeZAIR
meat	carne	karn
meat balls	almôndegas	alMOHNdəgash
meat stew	guizado	geeZAdoo
(to) meet	encontrar	eenkoonTRAR
melon	melão	məLOWNG
(to) mend	consertar	koonsərTAR
menu	menu/ementa	məNOO/eeMENta
message	recado	rəKAdoo
mid-day	meio-dia	MAYoo-DEEa
midnight	meia-noite	MAYa-noit
migraine	enxaqueca	eenshaKEka
milk	leite	layt
mineral water	água mineral	AGwa meenəRAL
Miss	Menina	məNEEna
mistake	erro	Ehoo
mixed salad	salada mista	saLAda MEESHta
moment	momento	mooMENtoo
money	dinheiro	deenYAIRoo
month	mês	maysh
more	mais	mysh
morning	manhã	manYÃ
motorway	auto-strada	owtooSHTRAda
Mr	Sr. (senhor)	sənYOR
Mrs	Sra. (senhora)	sənYORa
much	bastante	bashTANT
museum	museu	mooZEoo
mushroom	cogumelo	koogooMEloo
mussels	mexilhões	məsheelYOengsh
must (to have to)	dever/ter de	dəVAIR/tair də
mustard	mostarda	mooshTARda
my	o meu/a minha	oo MEoo/a MEENya

name	**nome**	nohm
napkin	**guardanapo**	gwardaNApoo
near	**perto**	PAIRtoo
nearest	**mais próximo**	mysh PROSseemoo
(to) need	**precisar**	prəseeSAR
needle	**agulha**	aGOOLya
negative (photo)	**negativo**	nəgaTEEvoo
next	**seguinte**	səGEENT
next (to)	**junto a**	ZHOONtoo a
never	**nunca**	NOONka
new	**novo**	NOHvo
night	**noite**	noit
nightwear	**Camisa de noite**	kaMEEza də noit
no	**não**	nowng
no smoking	**proibido fumar**	proeeBEEdoo fooMAR
not	**não**	nowng
note (money)	**nota**	NOHta
notebook	**bloco de notas**	BLOkoo də NOHtash
nothing	**nada**	NAda
notice	**aviso**	aVEEzoo
nylon	**nylon**	nyLON
occupied	**ocupado**	okooPAdoo
octopus	**polvo**	POLvoo
of	**de**	də
of course	**certamente**	sərtaMENT
office	**escritório**	shkreeTOHRyoo
often	**frequentemente**	frəkentəMENT
oil	**óleo**	OHleoo
old	**velho**	VELyoo
omelette	**omeleta**	oməLETa
one	**um**	oong
only	**só**	soh
open	**aberto**	aBAIRtoo
open market	**mercado ao ar livre**	mərKAdoo Aoo ar LEEVr

opposite	**oposto**	ooPOSHtoo
orange (colour)	**côr de laranja**	kohr də laRANzha
orange (fruit)	**laranja**	laRANzha
orange squash	**sumo de laranja**	SOOmoo də laRANzha
(to) order	**encomendar**	eenkoomenDAR
our	**nosso**	NOSsoo
out	**fora**	FOHRa
over	**sobre**	SOBrə
packet	**pacote**	paKOT
pair of trousers	**par de calças**	par də KALsash
palace	**palácio**	paLASyoo
(to) park	**estacionar**	shtasyoNAR
park	**parque**	park
passport	**passaporte**	passaPORT
past (beyond)	**passado**	passSAdoo
peach	**pêssego**	PAYsəgoo
peas	**ervilhas**	ərVEELyash
pencil	**lápis**	LApeesh
pepper	**pimenta**	peeMENta
peppermints	**hortelã-pimenta**	orteLÃ-peeMENta
perm	**permanente**	pərmaNENT
personal (call)	**pessoal**	pessoAL
petrol	**gasolina**	gazooLEEna
petticoat	**combinação**	koombeenaSOWNG
pillow	**almofada**	almooFAda
pink	**côr de rosa**	kohr də ROza
pipe (smoking)	**cachimbo**	kaSHEEMboo
pipe cleaner	**vareta de limpar cachimbos**	vaREta də leemPAR kaSHEEMboosh
plain (chocolate)	**chocolate preto**	shokoLAT PREtoo
plane (aeroplane)	**avião**	avYOWNG
plane ticket	**bilhete de avião**	beelYET də avYOWNG
platform	**plataforma**	plataFORma
play (theatre)	**peça**	PEsa
please	**faz favor/por favor**	fazh faVOOR/poor faVOOR

purple	**roxo**	ROshoo
police station	**esquadra da polícia**	shKWAdra da poLEEsya
pork	**carne de porco**	karn də PORkoo
possible	**possível**	pooSEEvel
post-card	**bilhete postal**	beelYET pooshTAL
post office	**correio**	koHAYoo
potatoes	**batatas**	baTAtash
prescription	**receita médica**	rəSAYta MAYdeeka
pressure gauge	**manómetro**	maNOmətroo
primus stove	**esquentador a**	shkentaDOOR
(to) print (film)	**revelar**	revəLAR
(a) print	**fotografia**	fotograFEEa
programme (cinema etc.)	**programa**	prooGRAma
pullover	**pullover**	pooLOHvovar
puncture	**furo**	FOOroo
pyjamas	**pijama**	peeZHAma
quarter	**quarto**	KWARtoo
quick	**rápido**	RApeedoo
radiator	**radiador**	radeeaDOOR
radio	**rádio**	RADyoo
rain	**chuva**	SHOOva
raincoat	**gabardine**	gabarDEEN
rare (meat)	**mal passado**	mal pasSAdoo
razor blades	**lâminas da barba**	LAmeenash da BARba
razor socket	**tomada de maquina de barbear**	tooMAda də MAkeena də barbeAR
receipt	**recibo**	rəSEEboo
(to) recommend	**recomendar**	rəkoomenDAR
reconnect (telephone)	**ligar**	leeGAR
recorded delivery	**registada**	rəzheeSHTAda
red	**encarnado**	eenkarNAdoo

reduction	**redução**	rədooSOWNG
registered post	**correio registado**	koHAYoo rəzheeSHTAdoo
(to) remove (stain)	**tirar**	teeRAR
(to) repair	**arranjar**	ahanZHAR
(to) replace (receiver)	**desligar**	dəzleeGAR
(to) reply	**responder**	rəshponDAIR
reservation	**reserva**	rəZAIRva
(to) reserve	**reservar**	rəzərVAR
restaurant	**restaurante**	rəshtowRANT
re-styled (hair)	**novo estilo**	NOvoo SHTEEloo
return (fare)	**de ida e volta**	də EEda ee VOLta
return (ticket)	**bilhete de ida e volta**	beelYET də EEda ee VOLta
(to) return	**voltar**	voolTAR
rice	**arroz**	aHOSH
right (correct)	**certo**	SAIRtoo
right (direction)	**direito**	deeRAYtoo
right in front	**mesmo em frente**	MEZHmoo ayng frent
river	**rio**	REEoo
road	**rua**	ROOa
road (main)	**rua principal**	ROOa preenseePAL
roast	**assado**	asSAdoo
room (hotel)	**quarto**	KWARtoo
round (direction)	**à volta de**	a VOLta də
rubber	**borracha**	booHAsha
safe (not dangerous)	**seguro**	səGOOroo
saloon (car)	**carro**	KAhoo
sandals	**sandálias**	sanDALyash
sandwich	**sandwiche**	sandwich
sanitary towel	**toalhetes sanitários**	twalYETəsh saneeTARyoosh
(to) say	**dizer**	deeZAIR
scarf	**lenço**	LENsoo
scrambled eggs	**ovos mexidos**	Ovoosh meSHEEdoosh

sea	mar	mar
seat (train etc.)	assento	asSENtoo
second class	segunda classe	səGOONda klas
see you. . . .	até à vista	aTAY a VEESHta
service charge	taxa de serviço	TASHa də sərVEEsoo
shampoo	shampoo	shampoo
shaving cream	creme de barba	krem də BARba
shaving soap	sabão de barba	saBOWNG də BARba
shirt	camisa	kaMEEza
shoe	sapato	saPAtoo
shoe shop	sapataria	sapataREEa
shop	loja	LOZHa
short (distance)	curto	KOORtoo
short (height)	pequeno	peKAYnoo
shorts	calções	kalSOengsh
shower	chuveiro	shooVAYroo
sick	doente	dwent
sign (notice)	sinal	seeNAL
silk	seda	SEda
silver	prata	PRAta
single (fare)	simples	SEEMpləsh
sister	irmã	eerMA
size	tamanho	taMANyoo
skirt	saia	SYa
sleeper	carruagem-cama	kahooAZHayng-KAma
sleeping bag	saco cama	SAKoo KAma
slide (film)	slide	'slide'
slow	devagar	davaGAR
slowly	vagarosamente	vagarozaMENT
small	pequeno	pəKAYnoo
small change	troco miúdo	TROkoo mYOOdoo
(to) smoke	fumar	fooMAR
smoked (food)	fumado	fooMAdoo
smoking	compartimento	koomparteeMENtoo
compartment	para fumadores	PAra foomaDOORsh
soap	sabão	saBOWNG
socks	meias	MAYash

soda water	**água de castelo**	Agwa də kashTEloo
sold out	**vendido**	vənDEEdoo
soon	**cedo**	SEdoo
sore throat	**dores de garganta**	DOORsh də garGANta
sorry!	**desculpe**	dəshKOOP
soup	**sopa**	SOpa
spark plug	**vela de motor**	VEla də mooTOOR
spinach	**espinafre**	shpeeNAFrə
squid	**lula**	LOOla
stain	**nódoa**	NOHdooa
stale	**velho**	VELyoo
stalls (theatre)	**'fauteuil'/** **primeiras filas** **da plateia**	foTəEEL/preeMAYrash FEElash da plaTAYa
stamp	**selo**	SEloo
standard (petrol)	**normal**	noorMAL
(to) start	**começar**	koomەSAR
starter motor	**motor de arranque**	mooTOOR də aHANK
station	**estação**	shtaSOWNG
(to) stay	**ficar**	feeKAR
steak	**bife**	beef
sticking plaster	**adesivo**	adeZEEvoo
stick-on labels	**etiquetas** **autocolantes**	eteeKEtash owtookooLANTsh
stiff neck	**torcicolo**	toorseeKOloo
stockings	**meias**	MAYash
stolen	**roubado**	rohBAdoo
stomach	**estômago**	SHTOmagoo
stomach-ache	**dores de estomago**	DOORsh də SHTOmagoo
stomach-pills	**pastilhas para** **dores de estomago**	pashTEELyash PAra DOORsh də SHTOmagoo
(to) stop	**parar**	paRAR
stop (bus)	**paragem**	paRAzhayng
(to) straighten (hair)	**desfrisar**	dəshfreeAR
string	**cordel**	koorDEL

student	**estudante**	shtooDANT
stuffed (food)	**recheado**	rəshayAdoo
style	**estilo**	SHTEEloo
suede	**camurça**	kaMOORsa
suit (ladies')	**vestido**	vəSHTEEdoo
suit (men's)	**fato**	FAto
sunny	**soalheiro**	sooalYAYRoo
sunshade	**sombrinha**	soomBREENya
sunstroke	**insolação**	eensoolaSOWNG
suntan oil	**óleo de bronzear**	OHleo də bronzeeAR
suntan lotion	**loção de bronzear**	looSOWNG də bronseeAR
surcharge	**sobretaxa**	sobrəTASHa
surely (of course)	**certamente**	sairtaMENT
surface mail	**correio terrestre**	koHAYoo teHESHtrə
sweet (taste)	**doce**	dos
(to) swim	**nadar**	naDAR
swimming costume	**fato de banho**	FAtoo də BANyoo
table	**mesa**	MAYza
(to) take	**tirar**	teeRAR
(to) take (film) out	**tirar (o filme)**	teeRAR (oo feelm)
tank	**depósito**	dəPOzheetoo
taxi	**taxi**	TAKsee
telegram form	**impresso de telegrama**	eemPRESsoo də teləGRAma
telephone	**telefone**	teləFON
temperature (medical)	**febre**	FEBrə
tennis shoes	**sapatos de ténis**	saPAtoosh də TENnees
tent	**tenda**	TENda
tent pegs	**espeques**	SHEkəsh
tent pole	**pau da barraca**	PAoo da baHAka
terrible	**terrível**	teHEEvel
thank you	**obrigado**	oobreeGAdoo
that	**aquilo**	aKEEloo

theatre	**teatro**	teeAtroo
they	**eles**	ELəsh
thick (material)	**grosso**	GROSsoo
thin	**fino**	FEEnoo
this	**isto**	EESHtoo
thriller	**'policial'**	poleesYAL
throat	**garganta**	garGANta
throat lozenges	**pastilhas para a garganta**	pashTEELyash PAra a garGANta
through	**através**	atraVAYSH
ticket	**bilhete**	beelYET
ticket office	**balcão dos bilhetes**	balKOWNG doosh beelYETsh
tie-on labels	**etiquetas para atar**	eteeKETash PAra aTAR
tight (clothing)	**apertado**	apərTAdoo
time	**tempo**	TEMpoo
timetable	**horário**	ooRARyoo
tin (of)	**lata**	LAta
tinted (hair)	**pintado**	peenTAdoo
to	**para/a**	PAra/a
tobacco	**tabaco**	taBAkoo
tobacconist	**tabacaria**	tabakaREEa
today	**hoje**	ozh
tomatoes	**tomates**	tooMATəsh
tomorrow	**amanhã**	amanYA
tonight	**esta noite**	ESHta noit
too	**também**	tamBAYNG
tool kit	**estojo de ferramentas**	SHTOzhoo də fehaMENTash
tooth	**dente**	dent
toothache	**dores de dentes**	DOORsh də DENTsh
toothpaste	**pasta de dentes**	PASHta də DENTsh
total (bill)	**conta**	KONta
tour	**excursão**	eeshkoorSOWNG
towel	**toalha**	tooALya
town	**cidade**	seeDAD
train	**comboio**	koomBOIoo

train station	estação de comboios	shtaSOWNG də koomBOIoo
traffic lights	sinais de trânsito	seeNYeesh de TRANseeto
tram stop	paragem do elétrico	paRAZHayng doo eeLEKtreekoo
travellers' cheques	cheques de viagem	SHEKəsh də veeAZHayng
trousers (ladies')	calças	KALsash
trousers (men's)	calças	KALsash
(to) turn	virar	veeRAR
twin bedded room	quarto de casal	KWARtoo də kaZAL
tyre	pneu	PNEoo
ugly	feio	FAYoo
under	debaixo (de)	dəBYshoo (də)
underground	metropolitano	mətroopooleeTAnoo
underground station	estação do metropolitano	shtaSOWNG doo mətroopooleeTAnoo
(to) understand	perceber	pərsəBAIR
underwater fishing	pesca submarina	PESHka soobmaREEna
underwear (ladies')	roupa interior de senhora	ROHpa eent ərYOR də sənYORa
underwear (men's)	roupa interior de senhor	ROHpa eent ərYOR də sənYOR
up to (time)	até	aTAY
urgent	urgente	oorZHENT
urinary infection	infecção urinária	eenfeSOWNG ooreeNARya
vacancies	vagas	VAgash
vacant	livre	LEEVrə
veal	carne de vitela	karn də veeTEla
velvet	veludo	vəLOOdoo
very	muito	MWEENtoo
vest	camisola	kameeZOla
vinegar	vinagre	veeNAGrə
visit	visita	veeZEEta
voice	voz	vosh

walk	**andar**	anDAR
walking shoes	**sapatos de passeio**	saPAtoosh də pasSAYoo
(to) want	**querer**	kəRAIR
(to) wash	**lavar**	laVAR
washing facilities	**casa de banho**	KAza də BANyoo
water	**água**	AGwa
water melon	**melancia**	məlanSEEa
water ski-ing	**ski aquático**	skee aKWAteekoo
way	**caminho**	kaMEENyoo
weather	**tempo**	TEMpoo
well	**bem**	bayng
well done (food)	**bem passado**	bayng pasSAdoo
what	**que**	kə (kee before vowels)
when	**quando**	KWANdoo
where	**onde**	ONdə/ee
which	**qual**	kwal
white	**branco**	BRANkoo
who	**que, quem**	ke/kee, kayng
wife	**mulher**	moolYAIR
windscreen wipers	**limpa para-brisas**	LEEMpa PAra-BREEzash
windy	**ventoso**	venTOHzoo
wine	**vinho**	VEENyoo
with	**com**	kong
without	**sem**	sayng
wool	**lã**	la
worse	**pior**	pYOR
would you like . . . ?	**Deseja . . . ?**	dəZAYzha
wrist	**pulso**	POOLsoo
wrong	**errado/incorrecto**	eHAdoo/eenkooHEToo
year	**ano**	Anoo
yellow	**amarelo**	amaREloo
yes	**sim**	seeng
you	**você**	vooSAY
young	**novo**	NOHvoo

your	**vosso**	VOSsoo
youth hostel	**albergue de juventude**	alBAIRG də zhoovənTOOD
zoo	**jardim zoológico**	zharDEENG zohooLOHzheekoo

FRENCH PHRASE BOOK
GERMAN PHRASE BOOK
SPANISH PHRASE BOOK
ITALIAN PHRASE BOOK
GREEK PHRASE BOOK

These phrase books, in a handy pocket size, will help you to be readily understood on all everyday occasions; to get you quickly and easily, where you want and what you want; and to enable you to cope with those minor problems and emergencies that always seem to arise on holiday. A pronunciation guide accompanies each phrase, the topic of which can quickly be found by reference to the contents list or index. Subjects include: customs, medical treatment, shopping, sightseeing, restaurants, cafés and bars.

TEACH YOURSELF BOOKS

SPANISH

N SCARLYN WILSON

With over 115 million native speakers, Spanish is one of the most-widely used languages in the world. This book has been specially written with the needs of the beginner studying at home in mind. No knowledge of the language is assumed and every stage is fully illustrated with examples and exercises. Pronunciation, grammar and syntax are comprehensively covered and the book will give you a basic, everyday vocabulary.

TEACH YOURSELF BOOKS